Enjoy your unfolding genius
every day!

Otto Siegel

6/25/21

Yes, You Are a Genius

Yes, You Are a Genius

Whether You Know it or Not

Claiming the Extraordinary Life You Were Born to Live

Susanna Lange
& Otto Siegel

Foreword by Dave Lakhani

Genius Press
Phoenix, Arizona

GeniusCoaching.net

First Edition

Editing by: FirstEditing.com and Judah Freed
Cover Design by Heather J. Kirk and the authors with Judah Freed
Book Interior Design and Production by Judah Freed
Illustrations by Susanna Lange

All client names in this book have been altered to ensure confidentiality.

ISBN-13: 978-0-9791102-0-7
ISBN-10: 0-9791102-0-3

Library of Congress Control Number: 2006938659

Lange, Susanna; Siegel, Otto
Yes, You Are a Genius / Susanna Lange, Otto Siegel

1. Personal Growth. 2. Business. 3. Prosperity. 4. Creative Thinking.

GeniusCoaching.net

Yes, You Are a Genius

TABLE of CONTENTS

FOREWORD

Finally, a book that describes how I feel — and I'll bet it describes exactly how you feel, too. But don't take my word for it; explore your natural genius.

Most people misinterpret what it means to be a genius. They attribute it to incomprehensible intellectual prowess or a complex understanding of more complex principles.

But it isn't — except in the case of those people whose genius is demonstrated in that fashion. Their genius is uniquely theirs, and yours is uniquely yours. Chances are that you've never allowed yourself to consider the fact that you might be a genius already.

But you *are* a genius.

I've never felt more understood or at home with myself than I did when I read *Yes, You Are a Genius,* and I never felt more complete or armed with tools to harness my true genius than when I finished reading this book.

In our over-communicated world, our genius is often blocked, or we turn our thinking over to the television, the Internet or the advertisers, and we stop responding to our own genius. We forget who we are, who we want to be and who we can be. And when we do, we feel (at first) vaguely unfulfilled, but over time we become painfully aware that we are not achieving our true potential, and then frustration sets in.

Yes, You Are a Genius shows you how to claim back your life and how to express your genius. It helps you break through old blocks that have kept you from reconnecting with your genius. I love the quote that Otto and Susanna chose from Buckminster Fuller: "All children are born geniuses; 9,999 out of 10,000 are swiftly, inadvertently de-genius-ized by grown ups." Nearly all of us are victims of that one single reality.

Admit it: You are a victim, too. I know for many years I was.

But as Otto and Susanna clearly point out, your genius didn't go away. Your skill and willingness to connect with it was diminished, but in just a few pages of the book you'll reconnect — powerfully. There is power in this book. And genius. It unlocks your brain quickly and it gives you permission to express yourself.

Once you unlock your genius, look out! The ideas, solutions, creations, and energy are almost overwhelming. It doesn't matter how well or how poorly you did in school. You are still a genius with ideas and solutions waiting to be tapped.

It doesn't matter if you don't think you are creative or smart. Your genius gene discovers what it needs to achieve.

If you've ever felt like something is missing, that there must be more, you need to turn off the TV, tune out the distractions around you and devour this book. Your starving genius will be satiated and you'll step onto the path to your true calling.

If you were one of the 9,999 de-genius-ized people Buckminster Fuller talked about, this is your chance to shake off the shackles of self-imposed beliefs, societal expectations and behavior patterns. This is your chance to explore your natural genius.

Don't settle for less than you were designed to achieve. Your genius is your promise and your future. Give everyone in the world what they've got coming and what you owe them — the very best of you.

I'm enlivened by my exploration, and *Yes, You Are a Genius* reconnected me with my path.

Will you join me? I look forward to our journey.

Dave Lakhani
Genius
September 1, 2006
Boise, Idaho
Author of *Persuasion: The Art of Getting What You Want* and
The Power of an Hour: Business and Life Mastery in One Hour A Week

GeniusCoaching.net

ACKNOWLEDGEMENTS

When considering who to acknowledge for helping us make this book possible, many names came to mind: Joe Bardin, who helped us bring our ideas into proper English and brilliant writing. Steve and Bill Harrison, who helped us write this book for you, the reader. All of our clients who continuously help us further clarify our genius concept, so more and more people can benefit and live their natural genius, and all of our friends who encouraged us to keep going.

But the real truth is that we wouldn't have even started to live our own natural genius if it hadn't been for three people: Bernadeane, Charles Brown and James Strole.

Independently from each other, Otto and I met Bernadeane, Chuck and Jim in 1989 in Munich, Germany at an event about physical immortality. Both of us participated not because of the topic, but because a friend had urged us to go. And the truth is, we didn't learn much about the idea of physical immortality, but we learned all about the living of it, and we have been learning more and more ever since.

In the past 18 years, Bernie, Jim and Chuck have made the biggest impact on us living our genius. They told us so many times, in so many ways, what a tremendous, unique value we provide to others just by living. They showed us the light when we were in the dark. They stood by us when our families and many of our friends couldn't. They made us feel our genius in moments when we were certain we had none. They never stopped telling us how valuable we are even when they went through their own difficulties. Bernie, Jim and Chuck are our true heroes, saving lives every day by helping people see how valuable they are by physically living.

They taught us how to see the value in people no matter what their race, faith, financial situation and emotional state of being. They required us many times to leave our critical minds behind no matter how "right" we felt in our pain. Their coaching and friendship throughout the past 18 years is the real reason we are able to continuously live our genius and to help others do the same.

Susanna Lange and Otto Siegel

INTRODUCTION

When I was 30 years old, I was walking in the beautiful Botanical Gardens in Munich, Germany, with my boyfriend, Otto. It was a lovely spring day, and all the flowers were starting to bloom in a variety of glorious colors. Otto and I had only recently met, and we were excited about sharing dreams about our future as well as our similar likes and dislikes. After enjoying several hours of intimate conversation, Otto suddenly spoke one simple sentence to me. What he said shocked and surprised me, and I eventually ended up spending several years thinking about it. I lost many nights of sleep pondering those five words, which eventually lead me to my current profession.

Otto said, “Susanna, you are extremely smart.”

He spoke those simple words with natural calmness and sincerity.

This doesn’t seem like such an unusual sentence. Lots of people are smart, so why not me? Why would it shock me and cause me to stay up at night?

I started elementary school in a small town in Germany called Dornstetten. The town was about 750 years old, and the 3,000 people living there seemed to have been there for the same length of time. Children would take over their parents’ businesses and then pass them on to their children, generation after generation. It was a 10-minute walk from my home to the school, a big school with many classrooms and lots of children — at least, that’s how it seemed to me then. Most of the children came from the surrounding villages. These villages were even smaller and seemed even older than my town.

Like most children, I was excited to start school. Unfortunately, I soon found out that I had a hard time connecting with other children. I was alone most of the time. I ate my lunch alone. I walked home alone. I rarely spoke to the very shy neighbor who sat next to me in all the lessons. Learning, which had seemed so exciting at first, wasn't so great after all. What the teachers talked about didn't make any sense to me, no matter how they taught it. This made me feel even lonelier. I had to repeat 5th grade and stayed a C and D student through graduation, except for physical education and art, in which I occasionally received an A or a B.

At the university, things weren't very much better. After five years studying Japanese culture(a subject that wouldn't help me find a job), I realized that I was still far away from graduation. I decided to give up, and I dropped out without a degree. I started to apply for jobs from the newspaper. The first job I had was in a huge laundry company, doing laundry for hotels. After that I cleaned hotels. Eventually, I was hired as a receptionist in an advertising agency.

I was overweight, didn't fix myself up well, and I didn't have many friends. I was never recognized for anything in particular, and my parents never said that I was talented or great. At least I never had that impression.

So, when Otto said: "Susanna, you are extremely smart," I absolutely could not relate to the idea. This was the most uncomfortable moment I'd ever experienced. It was more uncomfortable than any low grade I received at school. I felt embarrassed, awkward and hurt. For hours, days and even years, I kept busy proving why he was wrong.

What I didn't mention before was that after working for just three months at that ad agency, I was offered a position as associate account manager.

I didn't know anything about advertising. I didn't know that a job like account manager even existed. I had no clue what my responsibilities would be. But I accepted the job. I started working in a small department. My new boss was a senior account manager and our client was BMW Bank and Leasing. After three months in this position, I learned that my new boss had planned a six-week vacation to Thailand, and I would be in charge of the department. This meant that I had to meet clients and discuss advertising strategies with them. I would then come back to the office, strategize with the creative director and come up with solutions that I had to sell to the client.

In our company, the creative team worked diligently in the background while the account manager was the only interface with the client. I did well in those six weeks, and I sold one ad project. There was no crisis, and the company never really felt that my boss was gone. I wasn't rewarded or noticed, but I successfully managed several projects in various stages of development. I handled millions of details every day, giving instructions to the creative director who had been in that position for 30 years, and I did it all well. I accomplished this after just three months of working in a position that I had previously known nothing about.

As my career progressed, I began to earn a six-figure income as an account manager, yet I still believed that I never deserved to be recognized or acknowledged. My experience growing up was so strong that it took a lot of help from many people to make me realize the truth: I actually was smart, and I even performed as a genius in many areas. My genius began to emerge more and more. As people helped me see what I could do, I claimed my genius and focused on it. I created a prosperous, happy and fulfilled life.

Through our company, Genius Coaching, Otto and I now help people take shortcuts to identifying their natural genius and use it in all aspects of their lives. It doesn't have to take years of trial and error.

After working with people for many years, we now know for a fact that everyone is a genius, and that means you, too. Once you know you are genius, you know much better who you are and what you can offer others. Knowing you are a genius helps make your business stand out in the marketplace and attracts higher paying clients. What used to be hard work now becomes easy. You can experience a relaxed intensity that doesn't burn you out, that instead creates the highest quality of life.

Most people's genius is not one profession or one thing they do best. In most cases, it is a unique set of genius abilities. When known, these can be customized and applied in different areas of business and life.

You may well ask yourself, *What difference does it make if I know I am a natural genius?* Your genius is always there, whether you know it or not. The truth is that it makes all the difference in the world, because when you don't know exactly what your genius is, you can't apply it fully. When I began to realize where I was brilliant and owned my genius, I started to use my brilliance all the time, not just occasionally. For the first time, I was able to be proud in my life. For the first time, I felt that I could truly make a difference. I felt that I deserved to be happy and prosperous. I could ask for the salary I really deserved, and I could accept recognition.

Previously, most of my days ran together in a bland existence. Now, I enjoy getting up in the morning, and I look forward to every day. I am having fun. I have become sociable and outgoing. The old days when I would barely talk are gone for good. I am a successful person with a six-figure income, recognized by colleagues and friends.

You can do what I have done.

This book will help you identify your own natural genius and how you can use it all the time for higher performance and more satisfaction in your life and business.

Susanna Lange

CHAPTER 1

You Are a Natural Genius

We believe that everyone has a natural genius, and that means you, too. For 27 years we have been working in Germany, in Brazil and in the U.S. We have found the same results everywhere.

Whether coaching individuals who have high IQs or average IQs, the first thing they usually say is the same: "What does genius have to do with me? I am definitely not a genius. It doesn't make any difference if I am a genius or not. If I were a genius, I or someone else would have seen it by now! I would be more successful or more intelligent, or I would have a higher IQ. And even if what you say was true, and there is a genius hidden somewhere in me, I don't want to know, because it only comes with trouble! Some well-known geniuses are weird or work too hard or are scrutinized by the public. None of that seems attractive to me. Most of all, this is probably just another sales gig. You probably just want to sell me something that I really don't want or need."

Yes, this is what we hear over and over again. But the truth is, everyone with whom we have worked has discovered a genius hidden in them. Once they were able to identify and own their genius, they could apply it intentionally, so they made quantum leaps in their professional life and personal relationships.

Genius isn't just found in the Mozarts and Einsteins of the world. It's also in you. Albert Einstein said so himself: "There is a true genius in everyone."

Einstein should know.

Albert Einstein was expelled from three high schools and was working as a low-level employee in the Swiss government patent office when he published his paper "The Special Theory of Relativity" in 1905. He went on to win the Nobel Prize in 1921.

Does that mean that you're on your way to becoming a physicist who changes the history of science? Yes, if that is your personal area of genius. What if it isn't? Well, if you try to be the next Einstein, you'll probably end up bored, frustrated and dissatisfied, just like you were at your last job.

Forget the images of what it means to be a genius. Genius is personal. Genius is a set of exceptional skills written in the DNA of every single human being. So, unless you are a member of some other species, you have genius inside you. It's as unique and as natural as your fingerprints, the shape of your ear lobe or any other physical feature.

Most of us have been taught that genius is only for a few, so we have been trained to overlook, ignore and even suppress our own natural genius. However, every one of us has had moments of genius in which we make something happen so easily and effortlessly, it seems almost by accident. That ease is a clue to our area of genius.

The Sweet Taste of Clarity

It's time for a definition. Perhaps two, because one definition cannot contain all there is to understand when talking about genius. So let's look at two definitions for the word "genius" and you can decide which speaks most strongly to you.

Genius: *One who performs at an unpredictably amazing level, seemingly without effort.*

Genius: *One who knows his or her unique set of talents, creates the perfect environment to express them and excels beyond all expectation.*

Another way to understand natural genius is to ask the question, "If you were baking a Genius Cake, what would the ingredients be?"

Get out the mixing bowl of your mind and the spatulas of your brain's synapses, because here is your recipe for Genius Cake:

- *Mix in equal parts of passion for life and hunger for excellence.*
- *Pour in a fascination with a specialization in your field.*
- *Blend in something you love working on intensely.*
- *Add something that's simple and obvious-to you.*
- *Bring together one part focus and two parts persistence.*
- *Combine curiosity, exploration and a willingness to shake things up.*
- *Finally, stir in help from others to help realize it all.*

There you have it — your recipe for a Genius Cake. Once you bake it and take a bite out of it, you'll realize that you've always been waiting for this cake; The taste of your personal Genius Cake will change your whole life.

The Ease of Genius

There's a sense of grace and speed about genius activities. Visualize a skier going down a beautiful, snowy slope. The skier is exerting himself, breathing hard, but is by no means laboring or struggling. He has gravity on his side. He has momentum. Before he knows it, he's at the bottom of the run.

In this same way, you can complete tasks at a rate you may not have thought possible. You can break the rules of how to do what you're doing — always landing on the side of ease, expansion and excellence. Other people can't understand how you do what you do, and sometimes you can't either. You're simply operating within your genius.

So if you are not enjoying your business or job every day, this should be telling you something. Rather than thinking you are incompetent, you need to realize that you are working way under your potential — that you haven't even touched your natural genius yet. Unfortunately, this is the status quo of today's workforce in general. For the most part, we are working hard to do the right thing, but we don't even want to know what we are best at doing or how we can contribute most!

If genius moments are so natural, easy, elegant and enriching, why aren't more people aware of their genius? The trouble is that most of us were never taught what genius really means. Even worse, most people have been steered away from their genius in one manner or another. We like the way the brilliant inventor and futurist Buckminster Fuller puts it: All children are born geniuses; 9,999 out of 10,000 are swiftly, inadvertently "de-geniusized" by grownups.

Genius is Not Hard Work

We can speak of this from personal experience. If you stop and think about it, you may very well be able to do so, as well. Here's Otto's story in a nutshell:

"In 1977, I was teaching an introductory chemistry class to 14-year-olds in Munich, Germany. The content was new to the students and required a different way of thinking. I did my best to help the students follow. I noticed one girl in the last row by the window reading a book under her desk. To show her she'd better pay attention, I put a challenging question to the class. She raised her hand, responded correctly and immediately returned to her reading. I asked a couple more questions. Same story. She answered and returned to her reading. After class, I asked her about the book that fascinated her so.

"She was shy at first, because I had caught her, but when she saw I wasn't angry, she brightened up. It was a book by the spiritualist writer Carlos Castaneda, and she gave me a spontaneous lecture on why I should read it right away. I was in shock. She had rebutted my belief that learning had to be hard. She had answered tough questions without even making an effort. Further, I had stumbled over my own genius, which is identifying the exceptional talents of others, and this just four weeks into my teaching career. How long did it take me to act on this? Oh, only another 18 years!

You see, I had a mortgage to pay and a wife to please. Above all, I had resistance to seeing my own core talents. No one had ever taught me to go that deeply into myself. Things always take longer when we do them alone.

But I can tell you that in the next 17 years of teaching, I saw the same story repeated over and over again. There was something that stood out for every student — a high performer bored to tears, or acting like a clown, or developing Attention Deficit Disorder just to distract themselves. Or a low performer hiding and embarrassed about not fitting in. Each student had an area of genius, but typically it was not a subject in school. School was way too limited for them."

The Difference Between You and the Well-Known Geniuses

The only difference between you and the people we've typically come to think of as geniuses is that they were more driven to pursue it, or they might have had more support, or they might have been just at the right spot at the right time with their unique abilities, so they couldn't help but realize them. For those well-known geniuses, expressing their genius was not a luxury. They had an intense need to satisfy their specific core set of capabilities. What about you? Here is where you can start. Ask yourself:

- *What is my unique set of genius abilities?*
- *Which environment brings them out?*
- *How and where can I intentionally leverage them?*

If you don't know the answers to these questions, your genius is still dormant.

But why would you even want to pursue your genius? Isn't it easier to simply try to fit in and be happy within normal standards? The answer is "no." Geniuses who don't live their genius often become frustrated on one level or another. They blame their jobs, their parents or other circumstances for their frustration. Unless they can nourish their core talents, they will never be satisfied. Otto is a perfect example:

"Until I gave up traditional teaching for Genius Coaching, I was never really at ease. I heard that little voice constantly, 'There must be something more than this.' I was full of complaints about the school, the system and the world at large.

"Once I finally came to understand my genius, my resentment of school and society evaporated. I started working as an educational consultant with the natural genius of smart children. Parents came with intelligent kids who couldn't function in school. The assumption was that these children were slow learners, when in fact they were too fast. They first needed to learn how to slow down before they could excel at school.

"School could only provide about 10 percent of the stimulation these kids needed. The rest had to be found outside of school. So, it was natural for these children not to engage fully in school activities, which they experienced as boring. They didn't need 'learning-aids,' they needed help in understanding their own exceptional talents and then figuring out a strategy, with their parents, how to exercise these talents.

"I worked with children and young adults, typically from 6 to 22. It was amazing to see these children turn their lives around. But an even more remarkable phenomenon emerged from this transformation. Their parents started coming to me for help, too. They felt they also had exceptional talents that they had never learned how to use. This was when my understanding of genius began to be clarified.

"It's not just the kids who do brilliantly in school. And it's not just those who do horribly. Genius is in every single person. This realization was breathtaking for me."

Put Your Unique Set of Genius Abilities to Work

Genius is the expression of our unique set of exceptional abilities. The trouble is that we don't always take the time or have the encouragement to find out what those genius abilities really are. Often, we are drawn to a particular area of work that somehow helps us bring out our genius, but unless we intentionally dial in, we remain on the periphery of our genius and never hit the bull's-eye.

If you are one of the many who doesn't really know your unique set of exceptional abilities, review the following list of five clues for natural genius. Think about what you do that fits any of these criteria, and you can start glimpsing what your genius might be.

Five Clues for Natural Genius

1. You do it easily.
2. You feel a deep satisfaction.
3. You are recognized with a natural authority.
4. You dismiss acknowledgement easily because you seem to do it too effortlessly.
5. You don't understand when others have a much harder time doing the same thing.

Go through all areas of your life and examine them for clues of your genius. Ask yourself: Where did the five clues for my natural genius come out?

- *With which particular group of people?*
- *When I was a small child?*
- *When I was a teenager?*
- *When I was at school or college?*
- *When I am doing business?*
- *When I am with my family and friends?*
- *When I was performing a particular job?*
- *When I was absorbed in a hobby?*

In Otto's case, teaching allowed him to be in the neighborhood of his natural genius without actually pursuing it. To go all the way with his genius, he had to risk stepping out of the school system to start his own consulting practice. Genius doesn't fit into all the neat little professional categories that already exist any more than it fits into the subjects taught in school. Genius is so personal that it cannot be mass-produced or satisfied in a standardized way. Genius has to make its own place in the world. That truth alone is enough to stop most of us in our tracks, but we still hear that inner voice insisting: "There must be something more than this."

For example, Marcia came to us for coaching in "Frustration Management." She was a highly successful vice president of operations for a healthcare marketing company, yet she was tired of the day-to-day grind of putting out fires and of giving so much of herself to an organization she really didn't believe in. Even though many people work for companies they don't truly believe in, it bothered Marcia a lot, and that caught our attention.

We discovered that Marcia is a certified herbalist and a master in the healing art of Reiki. Ironically, she had always considered these talents as side interests. Without even knowing it, she had built a career in the healthcare industry bringing her close to her true genius — helping people reveal their self-healing powers. Now she is developing a new business based on her passion. Although the work is challenging and even scary at times, she is operating according to her true genius.

Now Marcia is skiing downhill.

A Bigger Game is Easier than a Small One

Genius needs the right environment to express itself. If you play a game that is too small, your genius has no reason to show up. If you play a game that is too big, you tend to freeze, and your genius abilities can't express themselves.

Finding the right playground for your genius is absolutely essential. You can be smart, experienced and talented, but if you have a business or job that doesn't require your intelligence and experience and talents, these traits can atrophy.

Susanna experienced this firsthand:

"My first job in corporate America was as an administrative assistant. I had had a successful career as an account manager in Germany, and I had coached children to achieve better performance levels in school. Most of those skills were not required in the administrative assistant position. In fact, my own way of thinking was considered a fault. As the assistant, I had to follow someone else's agenda instead of my own. I had to be good at proofreading and grammar, and I had to do tons of details without ever really knowing why. I did not do well in this position, and for sure my genius didn't show itself to me or to the people around me. Luckily, I was able to move on to greater playgrounds soon after that."

Desire: The Fuel for Genius

While your genius is as unique as your DNA, there are traits commonly shared by all people who are manifesting their genius. Primarily, each one has a bone-deep desire to challenge their exceptional abilities and develop them. This passion carries them through barriers and brings them in contact with others who will encourage them.

In the case of Mozart, his father supported him from the start. This enabled a much faster development of his genius. Consequently, by the age of six, Mozart was performing on the piano, and at the age of ten, he began composing. Few are so fortunate to have our genius made apparent and nurtured at such an early age.

The Payoff of Passion

Genius stays hidden because most people never learn what is their genius. Instead, they perform on the periphery of their genius, but not in the core. This impacts more than their enjoyment; it affects their earning power. Genius is often associated with sacrifice, but the opposite is true. Those who resist their genius pay the greatest price by working in jobs just to cover their bills, but never truly prospering.

Manifesting your genius means learning what it is, applying your genius in a field that matches it and benefiting by becoming an expert or specialist. In the professional marketplace, the specialists command the highest fees. They also love their work. Geniuses are not satisfied with just paying their bills. They may enjoy their lifestyle, but they don't live for it. Why? They are fully alive in doing work that means something to them.

Many of us sleepwalk through our work, driven by the need for financial security or recognition, but not satisfying our core passion. Geniuses are on fire. They are positioned to be the most successful people in the world. Geniuses can measure their reward in terms of income, quality of life and personal satisfaction. It's quite a compelling equation.

The Spark of Common Sense

When you look clearly, you can see that natural genius is simple. Genius doesn't get all tied up in analysis paralysis, where you scrutinize a topic, event, emotion, or person to such an extent that you get stuck. Any action or creative thought is stymied when your brain goes around in endless loops. That's because the brain's ability to shift from input mode (examination) into output mode (action) never happens. It's like driving down an endless on-ramp but never reaching the highway.

When you hit your natural genius stride, you often bypass analysis entirely. I recently spoke to a businessman who established a restaurant franchise and is now selling them all over the country. I asked him what makes some people buy his franchise and not other franchises. He mentioned the price and value of the offering, but then he stopped and said that many of the people who end up buying his franchise say they do so because "it just feels right" to them. This might sound reckless or irresponsible, but his franchisees are typically experienced investors. This is the entrepreneurial genius in action. Many of us get "gut feelings" about doing some sort of business, but the entrepreneur has the confidence and wisdom to act on it.

Ego: The True Enemy for Your Success

Natural Genius is actually the healthiest state for mind and body. Real genius and ego have nothing to do with each other. In fact, nothing blocks the emergence of our genius more than our own egos. That's because the ego is afraid to lose what it has, no matter how meager or unsatisfying it may be. Otto can use himself as an example:

"In Germany, being a teacher is a good and well-respected profession with a great salary and guaranteed employment. So, instead of moving on to Genius Coaching sooner, I struggled to be the best teacher I could be. I was never happy, but my ego was afraid of losing my status. Teaching was well accepted. I received a lot of recognition but very little satisfaction, and not a Euro more for all my efforts. To give up all that in order to work at something innovative and unproven was daunting. In the end, though, my natural genius urge won out."

Ego also enters the picture when a person develops his or her specialty area to a genius level and then automatically assumes that they can perform at that level in other non-related areas as well, not recognizing the boundaries of their talents. Salvador Dali was a genius. He began surrealism as a new style in painting. His art broke existing perceptions of what painting could be. But as a businessman, he was a mess. He almost ruined himself, thinking he was as brilliant at business as he was at painting. Fortunately for him, he married a woman who took over and saved his business affairs.

Geniuses usually don't operate by themselves. They require the support, nurturing, and, yes, the natural genius of others. Under the old interpretation of genius, they are loners who operate in isolation, removed from a world that can't understand them. Our culture idealizes the myth that only a few geniuses exist and these are super heroes to be put on pedestals.

This old ego-building myth has nothing to do with the reality of a true genius — one who exceeds commonly held standards in his or her area of expertise and who needs others supporting him or her on a daily basis.

The loner genius is often held to be on the verge of madness. But what triggers mental disease is not genius; rather, it's the resistance to one's natural genius and the isolation that often accompanies it.

This is why genius is truly the healthiest state for mind and body to be in. Genius is not a professional ego trip, it's the end of the ego trip.

Genius: Your Personal Goldmine

Genius comes with responsibility and accountability. If you don't take action you pay a price. You might get away with a mediocre life for quite a while, but there's a deep unhappiness that's always present. Even when you're happy, you're unhappy.

Your natural genius is not a burden; it's your goldmine. Sometimes you have to dig deep. Usually you have to remove some rocks and earth to get to the gold. The longer you've been here, the more layers there may be to remove. The point is not to focus on the worthless dirt and rock. Keep your eyes open for the glint of gold. Your genius is in you. You just have to get clear about what you're seeking.

CHAPTER 2

Genius Moments: Create More Miracles in Your Everyday Life

One way to recognize your natural genius is to see the bursts of exceptional ability everyone experiences in the normal course of life. We all have moments of genius, but we often don't recognize them. *Genius moments* are times when we let down our guard and allow our brilliance to interrupt the mundane life we have assigned to ourselves. A special ability sneaks out of us that we can't explain to anyone, least of all to ourselves. In these moments, the clutter and negativity of our mind get quiet. The stars seem to align in our favor, but it's really not the stars. It's our emotions, desires, talents and environment. When all these factors fall into place, natural genius happens.

For some people, genius moments occur only rarely. This doesn't have to be the case. We have helped our coaching clients radically increase their rate of genius moments. This tells us that with the right intentions, awareness, and environment, we can generate many more genius moments than we might otherwise experience.

> *"Everyone is a genius at least once a year; a real genius has his original ideas closer together."*
>
> — G.C. Lichtenberg, German physicist and writer, 1742-1799.

Unfortunately, the less often genius moments occur, the less we generally understand them, and the less we know how to make the most of them.

When a genius moment happens, go with it. Don't interrupt genius moments just because they catch you off guard or you can't quite figure them out. Go with the flow of your own genius. Afterwards, acknowledge what you've experienced. Don't call it dumb luck. Don't call it a fluke. Such statements are anti-genius propaganda that keep people in the dark. Instead, learn from those moments. Ask yourself: What was it that I did so well? What circumstance brought it out? What do I need to repeat that genius moment?

How Otto Did What Seemed Impossible

Here's a wonderful genius moment that Otto will never forget.

"In 1980, I was a member of a West German windsurfing team. We were invited to compete in an international event against Italian and French teams. The races were held on the Sardinian Coast in the Mediterranean. The competition was intense. In fact, the French and Italian teams were much better prepared than we were. They pushed us hard, and we had to go beyond ourselves just to stay in the race with them.

"After one of these really tough races, I was exhausted. I'd gone beyond my normal limits. After stowing my windsurf gear one afternoon, I went inside the resort hosting the event. It was my birthday, so I felt like having a drink.

"The resort's bar wasn't open yet to serve drinks. Instead of backing off and being the law-abiding teacher I knew myself to be, I went behind the bar and fixed myself a gin and tonic. This is something I ordinarily would never have done. Other guests in the hotel noticed me in the bar and wanted to come in for drinks themselves. Instead of becoming self-conscious and telling the guests the bar was really closed and retreating back to my proper place, I welcomed them with jokes and offers of drinks.

"You have to understand that I did not recognize this gregarious guy taking drink orders. Normally, I was very quiet and reserved. Yet I'd already gone beyond myself in the competition, and now I went beyond myself in the arena that really mattered to me — people. I was starving to connect with people and bring them together. Although I was introverted in my behavior, I was really a suppressed extrovert!

"The guests knew I wasn't the real bartender, but they were carried along by my own enthusiastic energy. We were all having a fantastic time together. Even when the real bartender came in, he wasn't upset with me. Like the guests, he sensed the wholeness of my intentions. There's no self-centeredness about genius moments. Everyone benefits. In fact, the bartender helped me make a drink I didn't know how to make and resumed his work seamlessly without losing face.

"Normally, my social inhibitions would have stopped me from even walking into the empty hotel bar, much less making myself a drink, and certainly not mixing drinks for anyone else. In that instance, my desire to connect was stronger. Instead of crushing this desire, I let it lead me past any obstacles I could raise. I didn't even know how to bartend, but I was ready to follow my gut feeling, and so were the other guests and the bartender. For the moment, it brought us all together in a fresh, joyful way.

"Could I credit this beautiful experience to my intense exercise and the endorphins it released? Was it the afternoon sunlight streaming through the bar window that struck me as so gorgeous and life affirming? Likely, it was both of these factors and more.

"In genius moments, everything lines up for you internally and externally. Your job, like a surfer who's caught a fine wave, is simply to ride the wave. In this way, you allow something of yourself to emerge that is normally kept hidden. In my case, it was my extreme sociability concealed behind shyness.

"What allowed me to reveal myself in this way? The extreme windsurfing challenge had stimulated my genius. My life as a teacher was so routine and I knew everything so well that there was never a need for my genius to show itself. I was playing small.

"I needed a big challenge to interrupt the boredom of my routine. I needed something to interrupt the negative self-talk that generally stopped me from expanding myself. 'Don't stick out,' I'd always told myself. 'Blend in with everyone else. I am a serious German. I'm not supposed to have so much fun.' That was the self-talk that held me back. Not only were these voices silenced in that genius moment, but it seemed as if they never had existed in the first place.

"Genius moments typically break rules, but usually they are rules that we ourselves have created rather than societal rules, workplace rules or family rules. It may sound overly simplistic, but it's true that creativity has to be creative. Genius can't be routine."

Love: A Basis for Genius Leaps

When people first come together in a love relationship, they tend to have more genius moments. However, we do not recommend love as a way to draw more genius moments out of yourself since the feeling doesn't last. There is definitely something to be learned from the phenomenon, however. If you understand the circumstances that give rise to your genius moments, you can recreate them on a regular basis.

Sandra had been a homemaker all her life. After she divorced at age forty-five, she wanted to start her own business. While she'd never cooked all that well, she had a passion for food and wanted to start her own elite catering company. When we asked her why, she told us a remarkable story.

Before her marriage, Sandra had had an affair with a French chef. She'd met him at a class she'd taken. He was the instructor. They had a whirlwind romance together. Her cooking got better and her French — which she had studied in college — suddenly got much better, too. When he took her to St. Tropez in the South of France, she was able to communicate nearly fluently with the locals. The trip was in October, after the summer high season and the visitors had left. Sandra had no one but French speakers with whom to communicate and she was able to step up to the challenge. Previously, she had never been able to speak French that well.

Sandra enjoyed an extended genius moment. She was in love with a French chef who encouraged her. Like many new lovers, they really didn't know each other well, so she saw few limitations in his adoring eyes. She was far from home and her own mundane routine, and out popped all the French she'd studied but never really believed she knew.

The trip ended and the love affair did, too. When she told us this story, we pointed out that that experience could still serve as a foundation for believing in her own natural genius. She'd expressed her genius once in the warm sun of St. Tropez. Why not do it again on a regular basis in her catering business?

She protested that she wasn't in love and she wasn't in France anymore, so what did it have to do with her now? Quite a bit, actually! When we're in love, we're excited, we're open, and we're stretching beyond ourselves to connect with a person. We're keeping company with someone who, at least for the time being, is extremely positive about us. This is fertile ground for our natural genius to pop out and surprise us.

We suggested to Sandra that she did not need to fall in love and be swept off to Europe again. She could feel that free about herself right now by choosing people around her who supported her. She could create the conditions for genius moments.

Making Billion Dollar Decisions in Seconds

Genius moments play a major role in business innovation. Ray Kroc, who built the McDonald's fast food empire, had his moment in 1954 when he walked into a restaurant in San Bernardino, California, owned by two brothers, Dick and Mac McDonald. At the time, Kroc was selling multi-mixer machines for preparing milkshakes. This restaurant purchased eight mixers and had them working non-stop. The restaurant served a limited menu of hamburgers, cheeseburgers, French fries, soft drinks, and milk shakes, all at very low prices. Kroc must have felt chills when he saw his vision of opening such restaurants all over the country.

He pitched the idea to the McDonald brothers. They had developed the concept of the modern fast food restaurant, but Kroc saw the full potential. In 1961, he bought them out for just $2.7 million, a sum that Kroc borrowed from a number of investors. He was 59 and had diabetes and arthritis. He'd lost his gall bladder and most of his thyroid gland due to earlier health problems, but Kroc went with his gut feeling.

In that genius moment when he first encountered the McDonald brothers' restaurant, Kroc connected the dots between the present and the future. He didn't create the fast food concept, but he saw how to bring it all together. From supply and operations to service and marketing, Kroc created a system that could be duplicated all over the world. Today there are over 31,800 McDonald's in more than 100 countries, making it the largest restaurant business on earth.

Genius moments are an opening to greater opportunity for ourselves. There were probably hundreds, if not thousands, of genius moments for Ray Kroc along the way, but it all started with that first exposure in 1954. If Kroc had ignored his feeling at the time, that would have been the end of it. By being willing to experience his genius moment to the fullest, he opened the way for all the success that followed.

Creating World Peace with One Sentence

You'll find history filled with genius moments if you know what you're looking for. John F. Kennedy gave us several of them. His speech in front of the Berlin Wall on June 26, 1963, was one. The Soviet Union had built the Berlin Wall as a way to keep people from fleeing to non-Communist countries through West Berlin. Mounting pressure by the Soviet Union was causing West Berliners in particular to feel more and more isolated from Western Europe.

In one phrase, Kennedy brought the American and the German cultures together. He let the West Berliners know they were not alone and made it clear to the Soviet Union in no uncertain terms that the U.S. and the West would stand by West Berlin. The phrase: "*Ich bin ein Berliner!*" In English: I too am a Berliner. His moment of geopolitical genius brought Americans and Germans together, strengthened alliances between democratic countries, and ultimately contributed to the end of the Cold War many years later.

Kennedy took an extremely complex situation fraught with political and military implications, and he simplified it into a four-word statement (in German). That is the power of the genius moment. It cuts through all the complexity that can distract people from what is really significant and touches us in our core.

In Kennedy's case, of course, this genius moment did not come as a shocking surprise or an instance out of character with the rest of his existence. Why? Because Kennedy was already awake to his genius for communication. He wasn't working against his genius; he was flowing right along with it. Ask not what your genius can do for you, but what you can do for your genius.

How Rudy Giuliani's Hidden Genius Prevented Chaos and Terror

Genius moments often come as a surprise to everyone involved, but they can occur by simply responding to our circumstances. Unfortunately, when faced with situations that require us to stretch, our typical response is to shrink back in fear. We duck our heads and wait for the storm to blow over. If we meet these more extreme conditions directly, however, we may discover capabilities we never knew we had.

How would former New York City mayor Rudy Giuliani be remembered if it weren't for his genius moments immediately after the terrorist attack on September 11, 2001? He'd probably be seen as a leader who had got things done but who didn't connect in a feeling way with the citizens of his city.

All that changed in the moments following the attack. Ironically, September 11 was a primary election day. After two contentious but effective terms as mayor, Giuliani was on his way out. The process of choosing his successor had begun. Instead of fading into the background, though, Giuliani was forced to take center stage, and he had to do so not just with toughness but with heartfelt compassion.

His friends have since argued that Giuliani was always a feeling person. That might be the case, but he had certainly never showed it much in public. The attacks of September 11 required him to step up and publicly reveal that strong yet empathic part of himself. In the hours immediately after the attack, the city and the country experienced a Giuliani they'd never known before.

Giuliani took charge, which was expected, but he also empathized. He let people know that he cared for them, that he felt their fear and pain, and that the institutions of the city would be mobilized to help them. He informed people about what was happening while he inspired the public to take an optimistic outlook. He did this not by denying the grief and fear people were experiencing — would have never worked — but by relating directly to it. He manifested a genius for communication and leadership no one had seen from him previously. Giuliani made it simple for people. In effect, all they had to do was listen to him and they felt calmer and better able to look to the future.

Where did this genius moment come from? Giuliani had it in him all the time. A more interesting question might be: Why had he not shown this ability up until then? In a *Time Magazine* article recognizing Giuliani as their 2001 "Man of the Year," he is reported as saying: "I spent my first seven years as mayor living out my father's advice, that it's better to be respected than loved."

Although Giuliani was successful, he never knew what was his real genius. It took an unbelievable challenge to push Giuliani beyond his limits to tap into this genius.

Genius moments are not so much discoveries about the world as they are realizations about ourselves. Given the right circumstances, what are you really capable of achieving? What hidden talents have you not allowed to emerge fully into the light?

You may not know for certain, but the genius moments you experience in life offer important clues. Begin to recognize your genius moments as they happen, and you are on your way to uncovering your personal genius. The more you know what you can do, what sort of challenge you need to reveal yourself, and what support you need, the more your genius is free to unfold. Then your genius moments are not just random any longer; you are now able to create them. Remember, natural genius is your vital right in the midst of your daily life. By tapping into your genius, you may not change world history like John F. Kennedy, but then again, maybe you will!

Cultivating Your Genius Moments

Please stop reading for a few minutes and take some time here to reflect on the stories you've just read. Did you see any common elements in all these stories? What stories resonated with you the most? Did you gain any insights into your own life? Please look within now and ask yourself:

- *Where did I have similar genius moments?*
- *When did I have them in the past few days, weeks, and years?*
- *What were the circumstances in which they happened?*
- *What was the challenge?*
- *What specific action did I do that felt like genius?*

1. What were your top genius moments in the past several years?

2. What were your genius moments in the past weeks?

3. What were your genius moments in the past 10 days?

4. What were your genius moments today? To help you become more aware of your genius, take a little time at the end of each day to write down your genius moments in a journal. Go over your day in your mind and ask yourself:

- *Which unexpected challenge brought out abilities I never knew I had?*
- *What have I done without effort that got me better results than I imagined?*
- *Whom did I connect with intuitively that supported me in my endeavors?*
- *Which brilliant ideas did I have that came to me easily?*

Share your Genius! Please submit your genius moments and genius stories to us at our website, GeniusMoments.com. You might inspire others by being featured in our next book, *Genius Moments: Everyday People Making History.*

CHAPTER 3

Physical Intelligence: You Are Much More Brilliant than You Think

Where does genius come from? The answer is simple: Genius comes from right inside of your own body. The human body consists of about 100 trillion cells. Every cell stores information in its DNA (deoxyribonucleic acid) and in its RNA (ribonucleic acid). Every cell is connected to thousands of other cells, together forming an almost unlimited information storage network.

At birth our bodies already know much more than we are consciously aware of knowing. Just think for a moment about a fertilized egg cell, the zygote from which you developed, and how it held all the information needed to create you as a complete body with 100 trillion cells. All that information stored in one cell. Amazing!

Now consider the synergy between your trillions of cells, more than the visible stars in the universe. All of your cells exchange information constantly through chemical messengers, enzymes, hormones, nervous system connections, and even photons, the smallest particles of light.

The human body is absolutely spectacular, but let's not get lost in the science. Let's bring all this incredible biology back to you. These intense cellular dynamics are the foundation for a unique set of exceptional abilities that form your natural genius. All this potential lies dormant until it is recognized and intentionally developed in a supportive and challenging human environment.

Your Physical Intelligence

Your cellular network has an unlimited capacity for information, ideas and creativity. We're endless when it comes to both internal knowledge and our ability to learn from the outside world. We call this inner universe in our body *Physical Intelligence* — a unique combination of endless information and wisdom for each individual.

Have you ever stopped to consider that your intelligence is biological on every level? Every thought you experience is a function of your neuro-biology. Your DNA, RNA and proteins are complex biochemical molecules that carry and share information. They communicate in three distinct languages: chemical messengers, electrical signals and photons. This sounds very complex because it is complex.

What's most important for you to know is that your genius is physical, and your genius is as unlimited as the interactions among the cells of your body.

The martial arts of many Eastern cultures have been tapping into Physical Intelligence for centuries. Each discipline developed its own technique to kick it into action through specific movements. Tai Chi, Aikido, Tae-kwon-do, and Karate all teach approaches to accessing your Physical Intelligence.

In Karate, for example, getting ready for a fight requires a preparation ceremony with relaxation and a specific ritual to get centered. Being centered is an extremely energizing experience that mobilizes all the mental, emotional and physical energies of the body for the fight. Even a five-year old child can break a solid pine board with his flat hand when this core energy is fully activated and centered for maximum speed.

Martial arts demonstrate Physical Intelligence in action. Meditation offers an entirely different way to access the same powerful core energy: By relaxing or distracting the busy mind, we get in touch with the true energy, speed, wisdom and amazing power of our own body. Think about the power of your mind when relaxed and clear.

With help from your mother, you create a whole body from one cell without knowing how. How much powerful natural genius is there inside you, ready to come out, ready to be challenged, ready to create the successes that you were always looking for?

You Are a Natural Born Genius

We are filled with information about things we don't even know about.

Fact: If you were to become a vegetarian, your body would automatically reduce the amount of meat-digesting enzymes it produces. That's Physical Intelligence at work.

Expressing your unique genius is an innate function of your body. It's your birthright. That's why genius is so easy. When you don't resist its expression, being a genius comes naturally. You don't have to learn it. The results of your IQ test are irrelevant.

In sports, this automatic high performance is sometimes called being "in the zone." Geniuses of their game, like Tiger Woods in golf or Michael Jordan in basketball, not only transcend normal levels of excellence, they appear to do so without effort.

When asked how they made a particularly magnificent move or shot, have you ever heard brilliant athletes say that they had no idea how they did it? They can't explain it even to themselves. This is because their Physical Intelligence has taken over. Geniuses innately know how to tap into their Physical Intelligence; they allow instinct to get their conscious minds out of the way. They let themselves do the "impossible."

This is the true stuff from which miracles are made, but if we don't know how to be truly comfortable with our Physical Intelligence, we can shut ourselves down. Think of those cartoon characters who run off a cliff and stop in mid-air. They start falling only when they look down. We can do extraordinary things that appear impossible to others and to ourselves, but we have to flow with our own Physical Intelligence.

We can't look down.

Genius Intelligence Goes Beyond Your Brain

Sometimes it takes guts to go with a gut feeling, especially if it seems to contradict conventional wisdom. Genius doesn't come from the brain alone. You should know that what we call intuition, or "gut feeling," has a clear basis in biology. There are more than 100 million nerve cells in the human small intestine. Add to this number the nerve cells in the esophagus, stomach and large intestine. You have more nerve cells in your intestinal tract than in your spinal cord. Where else can you find such a concentration of nerve cells? Only in your brain. In effect, your gut is a second brain, and it is the home to tremendous stores of Physical Intelligence.

All this is chronicled in great detail in a book entitled *The Second Brain* by Michael D. Gershon, M.D. In his intriguing book, Dr. Gershon quotes Descartes' line, "I think, therefore I am," then adds that Descartes only said that because his gut let him. The brain in the bowel has got to work right or no one will have the luxury to think at all.

The brain in your head is a wonderful organ, but if your brain is your only source of intelligence, you are missing out. The brain is overrated. Some people even think they are their brain. The brain is primarily a transmitter and receiver. It centralizes intelligence and organizes it in a useful manner, but it is not the originator of all your knowledge. For that, you need your entire body. That's why it's very safe to say that genius is not merely brain centered. Genius requires the participation of your entire body.

Genius Generates Unexpected Results

Action allows your natural genius to generate results, but these results are not always what you expected. Take networking your business, for example.

You go out and attend all the "meet and greets," then you pursue every lead with a well-practiced script. You also try some things on a whim, or so it seems, like calling a friend you haven't seen in a long time or giving a gift certificate to the kid who takes your ticket at the movies. Then one day you get a call from a company you haven't heard from in more than a year, and suddenly they want to start working with you right away.

Think about it. Has this ever happened to you? It probably has happened — time and again. What's going on here? While you were out there taking action, you were doing, not thinking, not over thinking. and somehow you struck pay dirt. You tapped into your unending source of Physical Intelligence.

Those opportunities came your way not from the places you logically anticipated, but from the physical energy you were putting into the world. You've shifted into a way of operating that treats all of life as one integrated system. You're tapping into your Physical Intelligence. You are greater than the sum of your parts.

Genius Creates Quantum Leaps

Several years ago, a four-year-old boy named Klaus from Augsburg, Germany, was brought to us for help. Klaus was passive-aggressive, and his parents were worried that he wouldn't be able to attend school because he'd either withdraw or get into uncontrollable fights with other children.

We were confident, however, that Klaus would be helped by a certain sequence of neurobic exercises designed to enhance the information flow between senses, brain and nervous system. In just three months, we turned his situation around entirely.

At first, Klaus wouldn't speak a word, not even hello or goodbye. Since he wouldn't communicate with us, we worked with his father, as if he were Klaus.

The pressure to respond to others in social situations appeared to be very difficult for Klaus; therefore, observing role plays between his father and us allowed the boy to listen without being put on the spot to respond himself. Klaus was such a bright little boy, he was able to pick up everything he needed by watching us work with his father.

We showed his father charts of how the body works in tandem with the brain. We didn't expect a four-year-old to grasp the biology, but we wanted him to have more of a physical sense of himself. When we look at ourselves as the spectacular biological beings that we are, this can help our Physical Intelligence click in more effectively.

We then showed the father a sequence of exercises that help the two halves of the brain work together. These exercises involved images, voice and physical movement to create sensory integration. We believed that Klaus' problem wasn't mental intelligence, but instead a disconnect between his body and brain, plus a disconnect between the two hemispheres of his brain, which left him isolated in his own world and unable to relate to others. He couldn't assimilate the world properly in order to interact with it, so he simply withdrew or lashed out defensively.

Klaus watched his father perform these exercises and then did them himself. This had a profound effect. His left and right brains came into sync, and he found he was able to interact with other people. For the first time in his life, Klaus could participate rather than just watch. What he had only imagined — being able to participate freely with his friends and classmates — he could suddenly do. He became a socially successful little boy, and we were thrilled for him. He just needed his Physical Intelligence wired properly.

Genius Simplifies the World

If genius and Physical Intelligence sound complicated, we want you to know there is actually nothing simpler. True genius is a simplifying force in the world. As Einstein said, "Any intelligent fool can make things bigger, more complex, and more violent. It takes a touch of genius — and a lot of courage — to move in the opposite direction."

Consider Pelé, the great Brazilian soccer player of the last century. He made incredible moves look easy. Known as the best athlete to ever play the game, Pelé did things no one had ever done before. How? By allowing his Physical Intelligence to take over. While playing for the Brazilian national team, Pelé scored an average of one goal in every international game he played. That is comparable to a baseball player hitting one home run in every World Series game over 15 years.

Look at Michael Jordan's record in basketball. At his best, the entire game seemed to slow down around him. He wasn't trying to process the game mentally — to think what his next step should be. He tapped into his Physical Intelligence: He was one step ahead of the action, knowing intuitively what to anticipate, and how to respond.

Genius is only complicated when you tamper with it, when you try to box it in, label it, and make it conform to some preconceived image.

Genius Goes Beyond IQ

As you can't measure the countless connections between your cells, you can't measure your natural genius. Genius is universally unlimited and specifically unique to every single human being. Can you measure Mozart against Michael Jordan, or Leonardo da Vinci against Mother Teresa? That would be absurd! The same is true of your unique genius.

Competition is useful to us in helping to draw out our genius, but in the evolutionary sense of survival of the fittest, competition is irrelevant. You don't have to struggle with how good anyone else does something. This kind of competitiveness actually suppresses your genius. Yours is unique. There is not another human being like you.

If you put Bill Gates on a basketball court, how well would he do? We all have a unique set of genius abilities that we can leverage as specialists. Within our specialties, we are as happy as children at play. Outside of it, we tend to struggle and compare ourselves to others, then we find that we fail to measure up.

A lot of people with measurable high IQs are extremely unhappy underachievers. Why? Because they are completely out of touch with their natural genius, which could bring them excitement, success, and joy.

Genius isn't complicated. Genius is your Physical Intelligence in full action without any roadblocks or barriers. Your intuition, your passion, your emotions, your mind, your desire for excellence, your purpose — everything is lined up. You don't have to think with your brain, the source of complexity. You're thinking without thinking.

Genius Speeds up Learning

The United States Postal Service (USPS) in Pittsburgh, Pennsylvania, switched its customer call center operations to a special keyboard that didn't cause Carpal Tunnel Syndrome. This innovative data entry system looks like a pair of gloves you slip your fingers into. Each finger is responsible for five keys. The benefit is that the tendons of the hand aren't used, so they can't become inflamed as in Carpal Tunnel Syndrome. The downside is that the call center staff had to learn typing from scratch. Otto was hired to make this transition as fast and effective as possible.

"My challenge was to help 100 call center operators switch to this new system in the least amount of time possible. Up until then, the system usually required two full weeks of training before people could learn it well enough to return to their previous level of productivity. That meant ten days of classes for eight hours every day.

"I introduced neurobic exercises into the training program for the call center staff. These exercises helped reactivate the connection between the left and right brains and to remove stress blockages throughout their bodies. These exercises included simple but purposeful physical activators such as stretches, breathing and acupressure points.

"The results were impressive. We managed to cut the training time by more than half. Instead of ten training days, these USPS call center employees needed only four. By removing blocks in their brains and nervous systems, we allowed their innate genius to radically accelerate the learning process. Now that was exciting!"

Genius in the Blink of an Eye

In his book *Blink: The Power of Thinking Without Thinking*, writer Malcolm Gladwell shows how most of our decisions are made within two seconds. This includes our business activities as well as our personal lives. According to Gladwell, we may take a lot of time to announce to ourselves and others what our decision may be, but typically we've made up our minds in virtually the blink of an eye.

Gladwell gives the credit to intuition, which is really part of Physical Intelligence. We are already using Physical Intelligence in many areas of our lives. By accessing this Physical Intelligence without emotional distractions or physical blocks, we can act much more quickly, intelligently and much more genius-like. Like most of us, Otto can speak to this from personal experience:

"A few years back I was driving home from the Phoenix Zoo when I passed a car dealership that was featuring a PT Cruiser. In the time it took the light to change from red to green, I decided to purchase it.

"Normally, I would have been more deliberate about making such a big purchase. But in this case, the car just felt like it was already part of my life. It turned out the car actually had more features than I imagined, excellent consumer ratings, and good gas mileage; that is, it had all the good points I would have discovered had I done the research.

"I trusted my gut and it paid off. I enjoyed that car for three years before buying another car in the blink of an eye."

Exercise Your Brilliance

Download your free genius training program with neurobic exercises: http://geniuscoaching.net/trainyourbrilliance.htm.

CHAPTER 4

Genius Blocks: Our Top 22

Let's face it. Genius is a loaded topic. We found this out very quickly when we named our business "Genius Coaching." One evening Otto went to a networking event. "Of the fifteen business cards I handed out, five were handed back as people said, "This isn't me." I wanted to ask, "How do you know?" But I didn't even have the chance."

Most people either don't think they have a shred of genius in them, or if they do think so, they are too afraid of admitting it for fear of looking arrogant. So, if you've been ducking your genius, you're certainly not alone — or original. In fact, here are our "Top 22" ways people escape their natural genius, presented in no particular order.

1. You're Too Busy

Who has time for genius when there are so many uninteresting, unrewarding yet seemingly important pursuits to capture our attention? No matter how unhappy you may be in your current career and living situation, the trap of "busyness" can be challenging to escape. Genius comes from the inside. The more you know your genius abilities, the more you will find ways to apply them. You will also find opportunities to fulfill your everyday responsibilities in much more fun and rewarding ways.

2. No One Ever Said You Are a Genius

School doesn't teach us how to identify natural genius. Parents don't pass on the awareness needed to discover and support genius. So how are you supposed to know? Everyone around you most likely is loaded with unrealized genius that they may never discover. Does that mean you have to follow in their footsteps? Of course not, but many do. Most people measure themselves against others. But since genius is unique, it can't be found in common standards. Who knows? If you step into your genius, maybe others will feel inspired to do the same.

3. You Didn't Do Well in School

School is hardly a gauge of genius, and that's not necessarily the school's fault. School makes sure that a wide variety of students receive a certain standard of education. Genius generally is too individualized to be accommodated in school. School is a mass production system. There would have to be a different class or activity for virtually every student in the building to stimulate every student's individual genius. So, the fact that you weren't a star student has no bearing on your genius. Forget those report cards and all the gold stars you never earned. They're old news.

Although attending school is essential for everyone, a formal education has nothing to do with developing your genius. At 15 years old, Einstein was asked to leave high school after his Greek teacher told him that he would never amount to anything. Einstein hadn't shown any interest in most subjects, and his teachers had the impression that he wasn't made for an academic career. His father agreed with his teachers and urged him to start a practical profession. Boy, were they wrong! If Einstein had taken their advice, none of us ever would have benefited from his genius.

4. You Did Do Well in School

Unless your genius is math, history or gym, your straight As were not an expression of your genius. The same is true of college, graduate school and a career. You may have received great grades all the way along and have created a good career. That's fine. But what do your guts say? If the mantra, "There must be more than this!" sounds in your guts every day and every hour, then you have yet to tap into your unique area of genius.

5. Mommy and Daddy Are Geniuses

The children of highly accomplished parents often opt for a more mundane, average living for themselves. This is because they measure themselves against their parents and find themselves lacking, so they don't even try to be great at anything. In fact, they often have an instinctive radar for their greatness, and whenever it starts to bleep, they head in the opposite direction. If this rings true for you, remember that you were never meant to live your parents' genius in the first place. You are supposed to live your own, so there's no problem of measuring up. It's just a matter of you fully being you.

6. Television

No kidding! TV can be a huge distraction from discovering your genius. Why tap into your own genius when you can watch other people doing it? Ask yourself how many hours you spend living other people's lives, stories, and emotions. All this time could be spent discovering your genius and living it. You could have your own adventure with your own stories, emotions, and feelings. The good news is that you would be in charge of the content and outcomes — not the program director.

7. Video Games

High scores do not count as genius — unless you're going to become a professional gamer (yes, they do exist) or a game designer. Unless video games are your area of genius, you may just be wearing out your thumb joints on a reward system that offers you no real reward. Put down the joystick and smell the roses. There's a real activity in which you can be great, in which you win something much more satisfying than digital clicks.

True story: One of our clients told me that she had to fire several employees at once for not getting to work on time. They had stayed up all night playing video games.

8. Health

Oh yeah, that! Chronic disease of any kind is a huge distraction from finding and unfolding your genius. However, some people require getting sick to interrupt their lives sufficiently so they can discover their genius. If you are one of those, please hurry up and get in touch, so you can get well. Geniuses do best when healthy, wise and wealthy.

9. Lack of Self-Esteem

Not good enough to be a genius? Do you happen to have any DNA in your body?

10. Lack of Encouragement

Natural genius does require the support of others. Some geniuses have managed without much outside support, but they haven't been particularly happy or nearly as productive as they may have been otherwise. For the most part, you need encouragement to stimulate and accelerate your natural genius. However, lack of encouragement is no excuse. (As you may have guessed by now, there are no good excuses.) We are each responsible for the human environment we create. If the people with you don't support you, stop sticking to them like they are the last human beings on earth. The world is full of people. Get out there and find some who will support you.

11. Career Advancement

Getting ahead is great, but not if you are sacrificing your genius to do it. Your natural genius can take you much further and give you far greater joy than fixating on your career. Too much outstanding talent is wasted on corporate politics instead of the tasks at hand. You may be good at politics, but there's certainly something much more productive and exciting that you're far better at doing. And if you're not any good at politics, be thankful. That's one less distraction for you to deal with.

12. Dumb Parenting

Like schools, parents usually aren't up to the task of cultivating genius. It's not necessarily their fault. Generally, they just don't know any better. There are exceptions, and if your parents nurtured your natural genius, then all the better for you. But if your parents weren't so hot at cultivating genius, why let that stop you now?

One of our clients was raised to believe that money wasn't important. Her parents didn't have much money, and they devoted a lot of energy in the home trying to feel okay with that unpleasant fact. As a child, our client internalized this lesson so deeply that she had difficulty with all numbers. She could never feel they were real somehow, or that they actually mattered, so she struggled with math. To get over her problem with numbers, she studied computer science in school, where numbers clearly mattered. She then developed a career in information technology. This woman knew she was missing something in her life. That sense of emptiness didn't stop until she'd cracked the code of the well-meaning but unintentionally dumb parenting she'd received.

13. Afraid to Stand Out

In Australia they call it the "Tall Poppy Syndrome." Here's how they define the term: If someone appears to be too bright, too successful or too happy, then people want to come along and cut them down to size. Well, if you're a natural genius and you're not showing it, then you are cutting yourself down every single day of your life. Some people may feel it's safer this way, but nothing could be further from the truth. Our own self-imposed limitations are the most dangerous force in our lives. But if you throw away the clippers, you have an opportunity to come in contact with others who are doing the same. Start standing tall. You may catch sight of others who also are aware of their genius.

14. The Boredom Trap

It's true that boredom can drive you to genius. Boredom usually shows up if you play too small of a game. You can be financially successful, live the lifestyle you always wanted and have the best family, but you can still be bored doing it. Unfortunately, many of us have been programmed to accept boredom. Unlike children, who have intense boredom intolerance, we adults often consent to our boredom, and we live with it every single day thinking we have no choice.

We mistake boredom for relaxation, but boredom actually is one of the biggest stress factors for the brain , since it makes the brain run the same laps over and over again. When we are bored, we use only certain neuron circuits. We get stuck in these mental loops. The more we use these loops, the more we choose them, since they are so familiar.

Boredom may be prevalent even in high-performing jobs. The moment work or life becomes routine, creativity shuts down, and you can become stuck in a repetitive process that stifles your natural genius. You may make some money, but you miss out on all the big things in life — like true personal satisfaction and happiness.

15. Denial and Disbelief

While it's true that many of us have not received enough encouragement, it's also the case that often we don't accept or believe the support we are given. If someone says you are incredible at something, why not listen? Why not take in the compliment and let it work in you? Compliments can take us places we have never been before, but often we resist them as if they were insults. The reason for this is that we don't want to be vulnerable. Let go of protecting yourself from what you think could be a false hope.

Also, we don't want to become dependent on the kind words of other people. Well, guess what? You are dependent on the kind words of other people! That's why natural geniuses need to find the right people and believe them when they tell them how brilliant they are. After all, they are just reading your DNA for you.

16. Waiting for Retirement

Retirement is strictly for suppressed geniuses. If you're waiting to retire before you manifest your genius, we have bad news for you — geniuses don't retire. Why would you retire if you were doing what you love to do and what you are truly great at doing? The beauty of your genius is that it isn't a hobby. It's a career waiting to happen.

If you believe you have to suffer through a career until retirement in order to enjoy your genius, you are terribly undervaluing yourself. Specialists always earn more than generalists. Discover your natural genius now. Find the right game that lets your genius come out. Become a highly recognized specialist in your field. Your retirement plans will quickly fade away, since your work and your life are far too much fun. The enjoyment from living your genius, furthermore, will help keep you young.

17. Just Plain Lazy

The "L-word" has to be addressed. We like to find a lot of complex reasons for why we don't achieve what we want to do, but one of the biggest barriers is basic laziness. Laziness is really the product of disbelief. Either we don't believe that more effort on our part is required, or we don't believe that any additional effort will make a difference. In either case, you are stuck. When you get in touch with your genius, you'll be so excited that laziness won't be able to touch you. The trouble is, you have to jump in first. You can't wait for your genius to stir you out of the doldrums. If it hasn't happened already, genius probably isn't going to change anything by itself. You must shake off the laziness to apply your energy toward developing and applying your natural genius.

18. Poverty Consciousness

Poverty consciousness is the insistence that you can't have the money you want to have. You could try to refute this consciousness with all the facts in the world about people who come out of poverty to create great wealth, but you will never be convinced inside. Your mind will always come back to you with the same answer: No!

Your natural genius, on the other hand, will say that not only can you be wealthy, you can love the process of getting there. Clearly your genius and poverty consciousness (if you have it) cannot cohabitate. Your head would explode. So, you're going to have to choose which beliefs will drive your life: Poverty, survival and mediocrity, or prosperity, wealth and accomplishment. Both are real. The choice is really up to you.

19. Modesty

Some people are actually embarrassed to be very good at something. They think it's wrong somehow. They dismiss all the positive things they could do for other people if they did manifest their natural genius. Interestingly, they also tend to be embarrassed to be very bad at something, so they work hard to carefully keep themselves somewhere they believe is in the middle. This balancing act is exhausting and leaves you with little energy for anything more than maintaining the status quo of mediocrity. Sure, you've achieved your purpose, but wouldn't it be a lot easier to just go with your natural genius?

20. Resignation

While geniuses have unlimited potential, their resilience has limits. We can only take so much confusion, rejection and disappointment before we give up. At some point, we have to see results, or we're going to lose faith. If you fall into this category, we want to encourage you not to stop. You are not alone! We are here to help you.

You may need to clarify what is your natural genius. The doors may not have opened for you because you're knocking on the wrong ones. Don't be too proud to adjust your vision, which may have been just a media image, a desire, or even something you are good at doing, but it's outside of your true genius. Genius does not have to live up to anyone's expectations, including yours. It just has to feel great and take you to great places.

21. Made Up Stuff

Over the years, we have heard so many excuses from people for not manifesting their genius. We'll just call this "Made Up Stuff" — MUS. When you believe something is a certain way, you create a rationale for it. It's as simple as that, but it's still fiction.

22. Emotional Drama

Emotional drama is a great way to feel intensity without actually addressing anything in your life of real substance. The drama certainly doesn't advance your genius one bit. Our recommendation? Leave the drama to the pros like Jerry Springer and stay focused on taking massive action to manifest your natural genius.

Juggling Your Genius Blocks

How many of our "Top 22" Genius Blocks are keeping you from recognizing and manifesting your natural genius? Here's a simple exercise to help you find out.

1. Pick any of the 22 blocks that may be a problem for you and write it down.
2. Describe one to three situations where this block apparently has kept you from seeing and expressing your natural genius.
3. Describe the consequences of stifling your natural genius in each situation. Be as honest with yourself as possible. Feel free to feel your feelings.
4. Pick any other block and repeat this exercise. Keep at it until you feel complete.

CHAPTER 5

Re-Connect to Your Natural Genius

When any Genius Block is allowed to continue too long, the block can often become a strong habit that feels almost natural or like part of your personality. Over the years the brain becomes wired that way. Being disconnected from our natural genius can be the one thing that we defend. Ironically, we may use our genius to block our genius, and we can become extremely good at this self-deception.

There's a tremendous amount of confusion surrounding genius. Some people believe it marks an individual as being overly intelligent. Others go to the opposite extreme and declare the presence of brilliance to be evidence of a nerd, a weirdo or an outsider. Some even treat Attention Deficit Disorder (ADD) as an expression of genius.

Make no mistake. Being disconnected from your natural genius *is* a disorder. It is an obstacle to the full expression and creation of the individual. In his early years, Einstein was obsessively rude and disrespectful to his teachers at Polytech College in Zurich. He exasperated his autocratic professors because he regarded most of them as irrational or ignorant, and he showed it. His independent, disdainful manner irritated and infuriated them. After the manifestation of his genius, this behavior disappeared completely and he turned into a charming and irresistible man.

Being disconnected from your genius can start early. In working with children who were troublemakers and outsiders at school, we have found that about 90 percent have above average rates of brain activity. They have difficulty in school not because they are too slow but because they are too fast. They need much more stimulation than they receive, so they create complexity to keep themselves interested. Unfortunately, this self-created complexity takes them away from what's really happening around them.

The Number 1 Reason to Disconnect: Playing Too Small

Playing too small usually comes with boredom. It might be hidden in the busyness of every day but it is most likely present when you don't feel excited about your day.

The first place most of us learn how to tolerate boredom is school. At school a lot of students manage boredom by creating virtual realities to entertain themselves. For some children, boredom produces both physical and emotional pain. Faced with such acute discomfort, they find ways not to feel it; they find ways to switch off.

By switching off the pain of being bored, overly active kids also put themselves outside of the social structures and activities of school. Separation from the other children causes more pain, more sadness, and sometimes even depression. They are tempted to withdraw even further into the constructs of their own mind. They might assemble multiple parallel universes to occupy themselves mentally in order to escape from their discomfort. Or they might become disruptive, like the class clown.

When growing up as a girl in Germany, my biggest problem was being bored.

Small village life seemed like an endless routine to me. My classmates' futures seemed to be laid out for them from birth. They knew what professions they would have, what kind of vacations they would take, what sports they would like (soccer), and what kind of marriages they would enter. I didn't know it then, but I was looking for something more creative, stimulating and adventurous. I didn't want a pre-determined life. That felt too boring to me. This was why I could never really connect to my classmates.

At school the subjects were too boring as well. When looking at a test, I could always imagine thousands of ways to answer any particular question. All of those ways were very complex, so I could never find the simple answer my teachers wanted. When I was writing an essay, no one could understand it because I wasn't able to prioritize and structure my words plainly. I would write the most complicated sentences with little or no concept of grammar. I could not even write a birthday card that made sense! So, I pretty much held off from communicating with anyone.

Most of my life happened inside my head. I daydreamed 75 percent of the time. I was definitely disconnected from what was going on around me. To escape from the boredom, I applied for a student exchange program at the age of 16. I was accepted and went to live in Costa Rica for one year. I embraced the new culture and learned Spanish in six weeks without knowing one word when I first arrived. After finishing high school I lived in Israel for a year. I learned Hebrew, worked in a Kibbutz and took care of physically and mentally challenged children.

Although I changed my environment drastically and clearly didn't have any valid reason to be bored any longer, I still wasn't able to connect any better with other people. The belief that I was different and weird was so deeply engrained in me that I took it with me everywhere I went.

This vicious circle only broke during that memorable moment when Otto told me, 'Susanna, you are extremely smart.' Although I didn't believe him at first, he had started me wondering, why could he have said that? And the more I asked myself and him this question, the more I could begin to realize everything that I had accomplished so far but dismissed. The more I reflected on this question, the more of my exceptional abilities I could see. The process was like fitting together the pieces of a puzzle. The more I could see this puzzle come together and see my genius, the more the feeling of being weird and disconnected disappeared. I now felt connected with the world around me.

We see the same thing happening with many of our clients. While they now manage their own businesses and can create exactly what they want, they still live the same escape they lived at school. A lot of adults who were under-challenged at school and who escaped school through daydreaming, playing video games and other virtual realities, we've seen, still do the same as adults in their businesses or jobs. The activities they choose to escape are different, but the result is still the same. They are playing too small.

Although they now have the power to change their circumstances, they don't know how to do so because the habit of escaping is all they ever learned. They still live their life more in a virtual reality than in what's real. They long for a life partner, financial success or ego recognition without ever getting it. They are overly positive or overly negative, but they can't face the facts. They feel other people matter more than themselves. They build others' careers more than their own. They create endless busyness without ever feeling satisfied. They have thousands of ideas but never make any of them real.

We see over and over that when our clients discover their unique set of exceptional abilities and own them, they connect to the real world around them. They find the perfect business partner or the perfect support person. They find the perfect clients, and they connect to the marketplace at large better than they ever thought they could.

The Number 2 Reason to Disconnect: Missing Meaning

Another reason to disconnect from your natural genius is the lack of meaning in life. At school, when we should learn the meaning of things, one of a teacher's most difficult tasks is helping us learn how to communicate meaning as distinct and greater than simple content. Unfortunately, most teachers are simply not up to the job. This is because true meaning requires an in-depth feeling about the subject matter and the work. Mere technicians cannot communicate meaning because they don't actually feel it themselves. Teachers are simply doing their jobs, and they expect students to do the same. Why learn biology? Because you are a student, and it's your job to do so.

Ask an average history teacher why it's important to teach history. He or she likely will pull out the age-worn cliché, "Those who forget history are doomed to repeat it." The teachers echo the cliché by rote, not explaining what those words mean.

A bright and engaged child might challenge the teacher by asking, "But doesn't history repeat itself anyway?" This idea is probably something the teacher also had expressed at some point, again by rote and without much enthusiasm.

At this point, unless this history teacher has a professional passion and can reflect some depth of meaning behind historical events, he or she will dodge this conundrum by turning the class's attention to learning dates on a timeline. Meaning will be left ethereal. Unless that student can turn to deeper learning resources elsewhere, she or he will be slightly less bright in that history class, slightly less engaged.

The appetite for genius is the desire for meaning.

Geniuses operating in their innate area of genius have no difficulty expressing the significance or importance of what they are doing. Meaning flows from them naturally. It is expressed in their words, excitement, commitment, and joy.

That is why as students we are drawn to certain teachers regardless of the subject they are teaching. We are magnetized to their connection with meaning and the energy this link-up produces. Why? Not only because they make the subject interesting, but because they stimulate us in a holistic manner.

History teachers who care enough to go deeper into themselves might arrive at the dictum of the classical Greek philosopher Aristotle. Man organically desires to know, and this is the reason we study history — to know, by way of the past, who we are.

This is pretty deep stuff, not necessarily for the students who ask the question, but for the teachers who answer it or look for answers themselves. The students may or may not be touched by the teachers' response, but they will no doubt feel the availability of meaning, whether or not they wish to pursue it.

Many times, disconnection is the outcome when people do not feel the availability of meaning. In the absence of meaning, often there is only blind routine, which leads to demotivation, which can grow into an addiction to something outside of themselves. Many disconnected people develop addictions like watching television, playing video games, or surfing the Internet excessively. What else is there for them to do in life? If there is no meaning in life, how are we to occupy ourselves? Our addictions keep us busy in lieu of expressing our natural genius.

In 1993, on a grey November morning, Otto received a call from his banker who asked for an immediate meeting. He recalled the incident.

"Two hours later I sat before him as he confronted me with an unpleasant fact. 'There is only one thing in financial life worse than being broke,' he said. 'It is ignoring that you are broke.' Quite a reality check! I had quit my job as a very successful teacher after 17 years. My new endeavor as a trainer and consultant was creating little income. My wife did not want to go with me into financial insecurity, and she filed for divorce. My children were deeply confused and sad. None of my friends and family understood why I had quit a well-paying job. They said that I was a terrible father because I could not provide for my family any longer. I felt like a complete failure.

"You might ask yourself, how can a smart person with a great education, a great job, financial success, recognition and hip friends, who seemingly has everything, reach such a low place in life?

"The answer is that what I'd been doing until that point never really meant anything to me. I'd been everything my family had taught me to be, but it didn't mean anything to me. My parents had wanted me to be a minister, and the only other acceptable choice had been becoming a teacher. I met my wife when I was 17. She was beautiful, smart and my first love. Marrying her just seemed to make sense. Earning a master's degree as a teacher with a major in biology and chemistry was easy for me. Getting accepted as a teacher at my favorite school seemed to fall in my lap, as well.

"Unlike the United States, teachers in Germany are well-paid, respected professionals. I earned close to a six-figure income and enjoyed the best benefits, including eight weeks vacation. I rarely put in more than 40 hours per week, and my contract said I could never be laid off. I was accepted to teach in a German government school in Brazil for seven years, where I earned more money and enjoyed more privileges.

"My friends were CPAs, teachers, and successful sales professionals. We all were well off, so we traveled to many exotic and beautiful places in the world. I always had a long ski vacation in the spring. Overall, I lived a life many people dream about.

"Along the way my wife and I had beautiful children, all of whom I deeply love, yet I could never be the father to them that I really wanted to be. I could show them how to live a great lifestyle, but I wasn't able to really give them me.

"I didn't even know what 'me' felt. When someone sincerely asked, 'How are you? How are you feeling?' I felt nothing. I didn't even know what they were asking me about. I didn't know that I could feel anything. What I felt hadn't been important in my life so far, not to me, and certainly not to anyone in my environment.

"The truth was that up to that point I never felt really happy in my family, in my job as a teacher or in my relationships with friends. I had lived the perfect image of what life should look like, but it really meant nothing to me.

"So, in 1992 I quit my teaching job to become a team trainer and leadership consultant for corporations. My parents, my wife and most of my friends were shocked. Far worse, I wasn't prepared. I hadn't planned the transition. I didn't get as many clients as I hoped. I didn't have enough savings to bridge the gap. That meeting with my banker telling me that I was broke took place less than a year later.

"My wife, my children and my friends were unable to go with me any further. My life looked too insecure and scary. And it was! Nothing I'd ever learned helped. I had to trust my guts and intuition to find my own meaning. Most of the advice I received didn't help much either, like how I should 'go find any job, even if it only pays $8 an hour.' I knew that every hour I worked such a job would have put me even more behind.

"The only thing that helped was a small group of people who didn't give up on me. The true friends and allies kept telling me that there is work out there for me, work that I could really enjoy, where I can be myself, where I could earn more money than ever. They were people I had recently met, people who seemed able to see in me what I had seen in myself when I quit my job. something much bigger and much more meaningful. I'm happy to say that Susanna was part of this group.

"Their encouragement and faith in my genius carried me through that dark time in my life. And what they predicted came true.

"One day, just before the new school year started, I decided to look for a substitute teaching position. It would pay me more than any other job I would be able to find, and it would take care of my immediate financial needs. At the same time, I would be able to keep building my own new business.

"When I walked into the administrator's office of the Bavarian school district on a beautiful Monday morning, I learned that a teacher had just decided not to come back to school because of wanting to stay at home with her new baby. She was teaching exactly my subjects, and the school was just 40 miles away from where I lived. I took the job and my immediate financial needs were handled.

"At the same time, I started a new business as learning consultant. I combined my experience as a teacher with my passion to help children get in touch with their natural genius. What I was never able to do at school, I was now able to do as a private consultant and coach. I was able to help children bring out their exceptional talents and their unique genius abilities, which helped them to be more confident at school and improve their grades drastically. What school couldn't do for them, I could.

"After my one year substitute teaching job was over, my business had grown so much that I could easily support myself and pay the alimony for my children. I was doing so well that Susanna was able to join me six months later. The genius coaching program that we developed together became so successful that word spread quickly. For the first time, I was making more money than I'd ever made as a teacher. I was much happier, and finally life made sense. I enjoyed every day and have been doing so ever since."

The Number 3 Reason to Disconnect: Lack of Human Connection

Individuals long for a human connection where they can feel loved, appreciated and encouraged — and where they love, encourage and appreciate others, as well.

A lack of feeling loved is one of the most common reasons to shut down, to withdraw, to feel worthless, and, of course, to dismiss any genius abilities. Many who have not felt loved in their childhood still carry on this pattern in their adult life. No matter how much they are loved now, they don't believe it and keep doubting themselves. Nothing they do is ever good enough, and they can never feel proud of themselves for 30 minutes or more a day. There always seems to be something that they could have done better or that they could have worked harder to achieve. But as we now know, genius doesn't come through hard work or measuring ourselves. Our genius appears when we perform exceptionally well without effort.

Just knowing that we should feel better about ourselves and should believe others when they compliment us isn't enough. We need more than information to change the pattern. You might need to talk about your situation with someone, what you feel about it and where you'd like to be. Or you may need someone to coach you, so you realize the truth deep inside, so you own it step by step. The key is to know you can do something about this habit. You don't have to be a victim.

Making a change can be easy. Haley, one of our clients, was great at school, but she was never an all-A student. She had Bs as well. Her father blamed her for the fact that she received Bs. He continually told her she wasn't enough, and she could do better. When coming to us in her 50s after a successful career as a financial planner, she still felt she wasn't enough. Especially when she would do something new and do it well, she would hear a voice inside her saying, "I could have done better. I am not enough." She constantly measured herself against others and always lost, because she never compared others to her strengths; she always compared them to her weaknesses.

We first worked with Haley to help her identify her unique strengths and her genius abilities. She had many of them. In fact, the more we looked, the more we found. We looked everywhere. What did she do exceptionally well at school, at college, in her first job, in her marriage, with her friends? What social environments would bring out those strengths? What was something she did well, and what ability came unexpectedly without warning? Did she do better with men or with women, and at what age? We scrutinized everything, and the list got longer and longer.

When looking at the endlessly growing list, Haley grew more and more impressed by whom she was inside. She had tears in her eyes. She couldn't understand why she had dismissed all the wealth within her until now. She couldn't understand why she had never seen it. She couldn't understand why she could see the talents in others but had never seen her own. She had felt disappointed when others would withdraw from her or not be open about their feelings, but she never saw that she was doing the same. By dismissing her natural talents, she saw that she withheld herself from the people she most cared about. After realizing that she was out of integrity with others, it became easy for Haley to change the pattern. She knew how she felt when others withdrew, and she immediately wanted to stop doing the same to them. She began to talk openly and loudly about who she really was and what she could contribute to the world.

She began to change all those things she couldn't do well enough. Dating, which had been uncomfortable, became easy. Selling her services became easier. Identifying her complete set of genius abilities made her see how exceptionally well qualified she was for her job. For a particular group of people, she could easily be an expert, and that's how she started to sell herself. Her self-doubts vanished, and fun took over in every way!

You can get only so far in developing your genius on your own. Ultimately, it takes a connection to others to help you explore and get clear on what is right for you.

The quality of people you have in your life determines the quality of the environment you live within. Why worry about air pollution if you're not going to pay attention to the human toxicity that may surround you, such as people's low opinions of themselves and you — expressed through criticism, jealousy, and dishonesty. This is a likely reason why your genius went into hiding in the first place, so you can hardly expect to draw it out in a similarly toxic environment.

To access your genius, you need to build the right human environment around you. Creating an environment where your genius can take root and thrive means developing relationships that are supportive. To a certain extent, you need relationships with people who are hungry to discover their own genius. They must be people you trust and respect, so when you present to them what you think your natural genius might be, you will trust them. You will be open and receptive to their feedback.

This may require you to attract entirely new people into your life, or it may just mean that you must go to a greater depth with people you already know. In doing so, you may finally realize why you actually connected with a person in the first place. On the other hand, you may have to fire some friends because they're just not up to the task.

Remember, you're not after a mere social connection, that is, a pal who shares some common interests. Liking the same football team isn't going to help much when it comes to drawing the genius out of you. You're going to have to pursue people for the depth of communication you can develop with them as well as for the dedication they will bring in propelling you to become your true genius.

As a rule, assume every kind of person is out there — deep, shallow, mean, kind, generous, greedy, etc. Get clear on the behavior you want from the people in your life. Start living this behavior yourself, and you will attract people with this behavior. There is no mystery here. We find what we are seeking. Sadly, we usually seek people only for a particular role, like a wife or a husband, a girlfriend or a boyfriend, or a companion of one type or another. Once we find people to fill those roles, we stop looking. That's why most people's pool of human resources is limited. None of the familiar category searches will work for your new purpose. Genius is its own category. If you orient yourself to this new way of seeking out relationships, you'll attract the right kind of people.

Take the risk to be open about what you feel. Create a comfort level with other people so that they can do the same with you. It's important to be clear that you are not seeking a mentor. A mentor is someone who has been there and done that. Mentors share their experience in a given field. You are not seeking experience or information; you seek someone who has compassion and a desire for your real self to come out.

Get as specific as you can about what you feel is your area of genius. Don't be too invested in what you're going to hear. A "yes" person really isn't much good to you. If you're off-target in your self-assessment and people encourage you anyway, you're going to waste time. In the long run, if you persist, you'll still get where you're going, but honest feedback is an incredible shortcut. Genius is all about shortcuts.

As a genius, you have a new need for people. So don't attempt to create the same old relationships you have had in the past. For one thing, you're not looking for just one person. Ideally, what you really want is a network of like-minded individuals who will support and nourish your genius as well as be able to receive your input to them. As you create these connection, celebrate your success! Congratulations!

There is an innate fear of going deep with people through the layers of sociability and mundane living to where genius lives. Don't settle for simply unloading your frustrations on people or having them unload on you; that's just another way of avoiding your depth. Expose your passion to the right people and powerful things will happen.

The Number 4 Reason to Disconnect: Daily Life Itself

Genius isn't something you learn. It's already there, written inside you. The trick is to remove the obstacles and distractions that have covered it up. One of the biggest culprits is daily life itself. We need to ask the question, "How do you gain access to your genius when everyday activities, demands and worries are so all-encompassing?" Time is needed to broaden our perspective, but with real life insinuating itself at every turn, where do we find the time? We can't drop all our responsibilities and obligations, but we can take some time to feel what is happening in our guts. If a voice inside is saying there must be more, what is it really trying to tell you?

For many people, one key to answering this question is slowing down enough to be able to listen. This is not always as easy as it sounds. One client of ours, an intensely driven realtor, wanted to expand her business, but she couldn't handle any more work in her brain. Like many people, she leaves her body out of the thinking process. Without this inner universe of intelligence, she was maxed out.

I asked her to get a massage once a week. She'd never had a massage before except after injuring herself playing tennis. Overly busy people typically only stop if something stops them, like an injury or illness. She'd tried yoga, which was torture for her because it was way too slow. She was a hectic person, and if the activity wasn't hectic, she couldn't see the value in it. So when she did yoga, she felt like she was wasting her time.

Like many people, this client related speed to productivity, but there is more than one kind of speed. The speed of ordinary life is superficial, task oriented, which generally leads to burnout. Rushing is one of the least productive states you can be in. When you rush, you are tense and mechanical. You may lose touch with the feeling of what you are trying to accomplish. When you *feel* what you are doing, you do it well and with enthusiasm. The speed of the body is unlimited. There's no burnout, no price to pay for performance. So, we have to slow down our lives to speed up our bodies, where natural genius lies.

Our client's goal in coming to us was to make more money with less effort. Many people wish for this, but what they don't realize is that they really are hungering for the power of genius in their lives. It takes genius to make more with less. For this realtor, her busyness was actually in the way of tapping into her genius and achieving her goal. After slowing down, at first with a weekly massage, it quickly became very obvious to her that she wanted a business partner. She did not want to do it alone any longer. Within a couple of months she was able to partner with two other real estate agents. She started to focus on the luxury real estate market. Her business tripled while overall she worked much less. She even found time to go on a vacation for the first time in years.

So, start by slowing down. Have no agenda for an hour and don't rush to create one. Sit next to the pool, take a walk, relax on your sofa without watching TV, or take a bath. Feel what your guts really have to say to you. You'll be surprised what new feelings and ideas come to you just by clearing the time and space for them to occur.

Create a Reality Better than Your Greatest Dreams

As individuals we tend to live in parallel universes — our inner world and the exterior world around us. We typically know that our inner life doesn't quite align with the world outside, but we don't always act to bring the two together. If we remain split; our inner passions and talents don't come in contact with the marketplace surrounding us. We never find out how to market ourselves fully and achieve our total potential.

This is a kind of dream state that needs to be interrupted. After all, we want to make money with our genius. This means impacting the real world. To do this effectively, we must allow the real world to impact us. That's where other people come in. We need to hear from others in order to make our inner worlds and outer worlds connect. We speed the development of our genius when we listen and respond. This allows us to take action and achieve measurable results.

If you keep to yourself, you go nowhere. Yes, you're talented, but that's where it ends. You must open your talents to the world and refine your direction based on the feedback you receive.

Often, our impressions of ourselves are extremely limited, as Otto knows. "I recently performed a training class for an IT company to sharpen people's presentation skills. As a foundation, we did a talent inventory. Everyone wrote down what they thought they were good at doing. Then they opened up for feedback and heard what their colleagues thought they were good at doing. Everyone had sold themselves short. After a discussion, everyone's talent inventory had doubled in size."

Meditate and Connect

Use the power tool of meditation to calm your mind, so you can connect with your genius from the inside out. Sensitize your awareness to your natural genius and start living your genius more and more every day! The style of meditation we use for genius awareness is different than most methods. Ours focuses on the biology of your body, the real roots of your natural genius. We call this technique Body Meditation.

Body Meditation: Connect with Your Natural Genius

The following guided body meditation is designed to help you get in touch with your natural genius from the inside out. To do this properly, you need a quiet room, a comfortable place to sit, and a companion to lead you through the meditation.

Your senses are always taking in the environment around you. This is true even if you are not aware of it happening. If you can't feel what is going on around you, the disconnection is not between your senses and the world, but between your senses and your brain. As we mentioned before, we learn to block out experience generally to protect ourselves or in imitation of others who block out their experiences. Even when we block things out mentally, we are still experiencing them physically.

Our goal is to re-stimulate sensory integration — the connection between your senses and all areas of your brain. It's better to be aware of how we are responding to our real environment, even if the response is negative. By fully feeling our response to reality, we can actually do something about it. Feeling is movement, so feelings automatically propel us to act.

Do not confuse feeling and emotion. Emotions, such as happiness or anger, are not the focus of this meditation. We are looking for actual physical sensations, like the beating of your heart, the pulsing of your intestine, or an image that may occur n your mind's eye that expresses your physical sensations.

On the following page, look closely at the image of the human body. Then have your companion read the following aloud at a slow, comfortable pace.

The Body Meditation Exercise:

- Sit with your legs uncrossed.
- Interlace the fingers of your hands, and let them rest on your lap.
- Close your eyes.
- Take a deep breath, filling your lungs fully with air, then exhale.
- Close your eyes and keep a deep regular breathing pattern going.
- Feel how your two hands are touching, how the fingers of the right hand touch the fingers of the left, how the fingers of the left touch the fingers of the right.
- Feel how two hands can feel separate or like one strongly-connected unit.

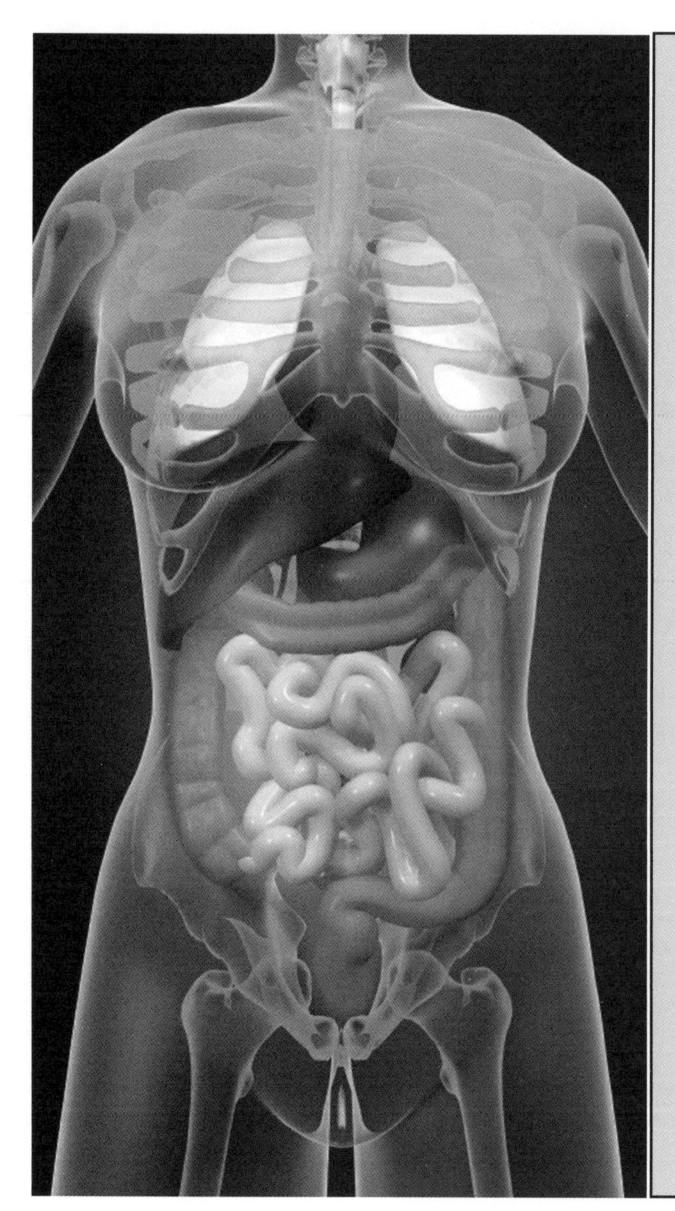

(Reader pauses for five seconds, then continues reading aloud)

- Keep breathing deeply.
- At the same time, you might experience the same connection that you feel between your hands, between the two halves of your brain.
- You might feel how information flows from the right side of your brain to the left, and from the left side to the right.

(Reader pauses for five seconds.)

- Feel your lungs expanding with a deep breath, and how air flows in to the right and left sides equally.
- Right in between your lungs you might feel your heart beating.

(Reader pauses for five seconds.)

- You might feel that all your organs are connected and working in concert like a symphony.

- You might feel the flow of information between all these organs and your brain.

(Reader pauses for five seconds.)

- Now feel your shoulders and neck and let go of any tension there.
- Feel how the information flow between your brain and body increases, and how air flows more easily in and out of your lungs.

(Reader pauses for five seconds.)

- Feel the environment around you, feel the air, hear the sounds, sense your surroundings.

(Reader pauses for five seconds.)

- Feel a current connection with people who are important to you, like family, friends and colleagues.

(Reader pauses for five seconds.)

- Take another deep breath to realize that all these connections between your brain, body and the world are real for you right now.
- Feel how safe it is to be connected.
- Feel how this connection lets you fully come out as the natural genius you are.
- Feel how it allows you to be in touch with your innate genius abilities.
- Feel how it allows you to express them to others just at the right time.

- Feel how these connections allow you to truly receive compliments and acknowledgements because they were expressed to you for the real genius you are.
- You might see a picture in your mind's eye describing these connections.
- You might feel a sensation like pressure, or tingling or just a deep relaxation.

(Reader pauses for five seconds.)

- Take three more slow, deep breaths.
- When you are ready, slowly open your eyes.

It's likely that by the time you've finished this exercise you will be reaping its rewards. After working with many people, and hearing so many positive comments about it, we thought we'd share some of the benefits with you here:

1. Experiencing relaxed intensity.
2. Seeing simplicity, no matter how complex others see the same situation.
3. Being quicker, faster and more to the point.
4. Asking the right questions so that new knowledge can be applied immediately.

To download the Body Meditation as an audio file, go to this website address: http://geniuscoaching.net/geniusmeditation.htm

CHAPTER 6

The 7 Core Benefits of Living Your Natural Genius

When you live your genius abilities to the fullest, the real you shows up in the world. The line between you and your genius disappears completely. You don't "have" a genius any longer; it truly becomes you. Being your natural genius comes with the best rewards: Lots of *fun* with lots of caring people, *speed,* seeing *simplicity* in very complex situations, *relaxed intensity, self-confidence, a passion for reality,* and most of all, *serendipity,* the ability to be at the right spot with the right people at the right time.

What exactly do you notice and feel when you see natural genius in action?

1. Fun

You truly enjoy what you do every day and feel a great deal of satisfaction from your daily challenges. You feel that you can move mountains and create lots of miracles on the way. Your unique and extraordinary expression inspires people around you and motivates them to show a positive attitude. You cause lots of smiles and laughter with your light-hearted comments that resonate with people around you. You effortlessly attract lots of clients — and just the ones that you always wanted. Others perceive you as an expert and ask, "What did you do to be so successful?" You learn how it feels to receive more money and recognition. You learn how it feels to receive lots of caring.

Jon came to us full of questions about his genius. He wasn't sure he was one, but he was willing to find out. After identifying his unique set of exceptional abilities, he now enjoys his genius almost every day. "Instead of beating myself up over procrastination or shortcomings," he told us, "I run with my exceptional talents and use them continuously. I have a smile on my face, even if someone around me has a bad day. I forget to be humble and secretive about my natural genius. I live it full out."

After being a business analyst for many years, Jon felt that he could express his genius much better in sales. This was a transition not many had done successfully before him, but he found the job. In his new position, he is not only much happier because he can live his genius much more, he also changes the company statistics daily. He won more clients faster than any other person who'd ever started. He took on challenges that no one before could. The VP of sales was so impressed with Jon's performance that he slowly overcame his doubts about genius and wanted to explore his own.

2. Speed

You just get lots of stuff done. You don't stop until you see results. You may forget the world around you while you are "in your element." You are moving fast, yet the world seems to slow down. High efficiency and effectiveness feel natural.

Look at what Jon got done. Jon not only changed positions, he changed industries. He had been a business analyst for a Fortune 100 aerospace company, and the sales position was in a commercial insurance company. He transitioned from a business analyst position into executive account management based on a personal connection he'd felt with his new boss several years ago. Their spontaneous reconnection actually was the only reason he'd made the leap. Within eight weeks he acquired a huge amount of new industry knowledge. Within a few weeks he had two major clients under contract, which was unprecedented in this industry. No one had ever before been able to acquire so much new information in so little time and shortly afterward close the sale on two new accounts.

Jon's speed comes out daily, but sometimes it's even more obvious. One day his boss walked in and told him, "I have a scheduling conflict. Our company has a suite for a dozen people at the ball game tonight, but I have a family emergency, and I forgot all about the game, so I did not invite any client or prospective client to the ball park. Can you step in and be the host?" Jon quickly replied, "Yes, no problem." Within an hour on the phone, he had twelve prospective clients committed to enjoying the ball game with him while he built more trust and deeper relationships with them.

3. Simplicity

The famous equation $E = MC^2$ stands for Einstein's genius to simplify highly complex thoughts and insights into mathematical terms. Now, this is a true hallmark of genius in action — to intuitively comprehend a complex picture and describe the core elements in a simple statement. It requires sharp and open senses, full presence and a strong intuition. Most famous quotes are created that way and achieve longevity as true pearls of wisdom over generations. Even though many people have used the same words before and since, the phrase, "I have a dream," will forever be associated with Rev. Martin Luther King, Jr. His choice to use that now-famous line in 1963 was a spontaneous inspiration as he faced tens of thousands of civil rights marchers gathered at the Lincoln Memorial. His genius deeply impacted the entire world. When genius is in action, simplicity is too.

4. Relaxed Intensity

During the Winter Olympic Games in 2006, the world of cross-country Nordic skiing witnessed a mesmerizing experience: — an 18-mile (30 km) men's race by the defending Olympic Gold medalist Frode Estil of Norway. Like many of the great Norwegian skiers, he was born into a world of snow, but that didn't give him what true champions possess, a different vision of things.

In the first leg of the race, Estil became entangled with a cluster of other skiers and fell down, breaking one of his skis. He now was dead last. Sports broadcasters covering the event live on TV said the race was over for him. Estil did not think that way.

Mounting a replacement ski, Estil began to chase the 70 skiers pulling ahead of him. At the laborious pace of cross-country skiing, in a span of only 15 minutes he passed them one by one until he rejoined the leaders. He still had enough energy for the mass sprint to the finish line. For most skiers, that's a full day's work, but not to a champion. Estil won the greatest silver medal ever, only 0.6 seconds behind the gold medalist. If you deduct the 45 seconds lost while entangled with other skiers, he would have performed the best 30 km cross-country ski run ever.

Estil demonstrated his genius to all. His performance seemed effortless. He never showed any mark of hard work. He smiled as he passed his competitors. Everything came together in his skiing — his expertise, precise training, enthusiasm, and an extraordinary challenge that brought out of him more than anyone ever expected.

We love to watch genius performances by athletes. They touch our core and resonate with our own natural genius. Every true champion shows relaxed intensity in their best performances. There's never tension or struggle. Going all out with a true passion to do the impossible is a natural ability of human beings.

5. Self-Confidence

You truly own every single DNA molecule in every one of your 100 trillion cells. What a big biological foundation for your natural genius! When you know your genius abilities and live them out fully, all of these cells are in sync. It's the most satisfying and joyful experience in life. When you don't live your genius all the way, you don't use your capabilities all the way, so some of your cells stay dormant. You deny them their action, so you will never experience the joy and self-confidence that you can experience with your genius in full action.

Your genius in action automatically attracts acknowledgement and appreciation from others, which will help build your self-confidence even more.

For more than a decade, Pete had been working with great success as a sales executive for a large chemical company, but he felt deep unhappiness. To break the endless routine of sameness, he started a sales coaching company and ventured out into the open market. One day he received a phone call from the CFO of a client company, “Would you like to come on board as the CEO and president of our organization?” Over the next few weeks, Pete researched the company, met the owner and his son, did his due diligence. He could negotiate from a position of strength and profound knowledge. His personal genius and background boosted Pete’s confidence that he could lead this company, which produced fuel cells. As a teenager, Pete had played with alternative energy solutions then graduated college with a chemical engineering degree. His successful career in a chemical company gave him the business proficiency for this industry.

Given this new opportunity, Pete’s natural genius came to life. All his genius abilities were required — his industry experience, management skills, business acumen, and innate brilliance in sales, plus his passion for reality. Pete had the best job in his life.

6. Passion for Reality

As we saw in Chapter 5, a lot of us disconnect from reality to escape uncomfortable routines and boredom. The truth is that reality is the most wonderful and best thing that ever happened to us. Geniuses are well aware of this. They know that they can make their dreams come true only when they’re in touch with what’s real. They know the truth about their real abilities. They know how they can give to others what they really want. They know that they receive money only from real people. That’s why they have a passion for reality. Geniuses are not optimists or pessimists because they are in charge of their reality. They clearly know where they are. They know where they want to go. They know what they need to get them there.

Our client Sandra said, "I cleaned out my house, both personally and in my business. I got rid of all my dead weight and I feel more alive than ever. Everything is clicking, from friendships to business and personal happiness. My genius would have been stuffed down, and I would have gotten along somehow, but internally I would not have been happy. The terrorist inside would have taken over. It would have been an OK life, but not a great life. My genius life is so much better and more enriched."

7. Serendipity

Genius serendipity happens when everything falls in place: The right time, the right people, the right environment — everything comes together like magic. For any genius, serendipity is a life style. Serendipity no longer is that rare moment created by luck; it's part of being a genius. You are now the star in your field of expertise.

Ryan came to us as an introvert teenager who actively disliked school. He was on the verge of dropping out because nothing made sense to him. After working with him for awhile, we identified that he had lots of exceptional abilities in business. He had a strong common sense for putting deals together. Now what? How could Ryan possibly be a businessman at age 16 while he struggled his way toward graduation?

Ryan's parents whole-heartedly supported him. They encouraged every business idea he had. Another client of ours, Ron, owned a vending business. Ryan's parents helped Ryan to buy a truck and several vending machines. Ron mentored him to place and service the machines properly, to run his business responsibly. Ryan now was happy. He was able to do what he wanted to do — business. The deal changed his entire outlook on life. Less than two years later another miracle happened. Ryan graduated from high school.

He could have spent months or even years seeking a business that matched his genius. The "miraculous" fact that another client of ours was able to offer to Ryan exactly the right business opportunity was a classic case of serendipity.

Visualize Your Natural Genius

Discovering the qualities of your genius is an important step. These genius qualities only expand as realities within you if you truly own them. We'd like to offer a power-tool that will help you to own your natural genius from the inside out.

Visualization exercises have been proven to work in a variety of applications. Athletes use visualization to enhance performance and recover faster from injuries. Among cancer patients, visualization has been shown to accelerate healing.

Let the powerful visualization technique below help you to become your genius more and more. As with the meditation, you'll need a quiet environment and someone to guide you through this visualization exercise.

Visualization: Unlock Your Genius

Find a quiet room, a comfortable place to sit, and a friend to lead you through the visualization. Afterwards share your experiences together.

Begin by looking at the image of the DNA spiral (right) for one minute.

- See that this strand of DNA is just like yours, and appreciate that thanks to modern science, we know what DNA looks like.
- Now close your eyes.
- Sit with your legs uncrossed.
- Interlace your fingers; keep breathing deeply throughout the visualization.

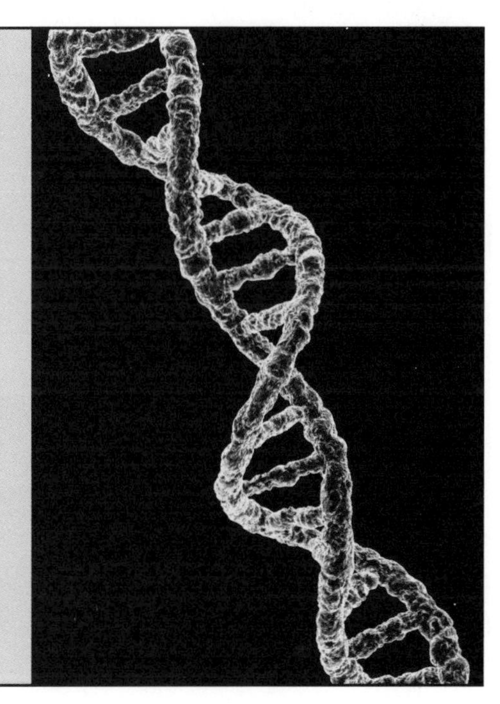

- Visualize the air entering your lungs while you inhale.
- Visualize one little cell in the wall of one of your lungs.
- Ask for permission to enter the cell and look around.
- Inside, you see a sphere, which is the cell nucleus.
- Looking closer, you can see an opening to enter the nucleus.
- Go through the cell opening to the inside of the nucleus.
- Inside the nucleus, you can see 46 chromosomes all knotted together.
- Reach out with your hand and bring one chromosome closer to you.
- As you examine it closer, you can see that it contains DNA, matching the picture you just studied.
- There's a vast amount of information here for you to observe.
- Most of the DNA is transparent, but part is covered with vanilla-colored proteins.
- As you remove these protein layers, dormant parts of your DNA become available to you.
- You see crystal-clear DNA waiting to be read, decoded into the feeling of your unique genius abilities, and translated into real actions aligned with these talents.
- This is where your personal genius is hiding.

(Reader pauses for 5 seconds)

- The cell you are in begins communicating with other cells in a new way, causing a chain reaction throughout your body.

(Reader pauses for 5 seconds)

- You can see the huge amount of information available to you which is the real source of your unique genius.

- Like a child at play, you give yourself permission to allow your genius to express itself without any effort or control.
- You can see yourself living your genius all the way.
- You can see how everything that you do is easy for you.
- You can see how everything you touch becomes successful with an amazing speed.
- You can see how it's simple to get the things that you want to get.
- You can see yourself creating what you want with an innate genius authority.
- Your self-confidence attracts to you better clients and team members than you ever imagined.
- You are always at the right place at the right time, meeting the right people who can bring you forward in what you want.
- Remember to keep breathing deeply.

(Reader pauses for 5 seconds)

- Cover the DNA that you examined with the protein layers that you removed earlier, so the DNA strand appears as you originally found it.
- Now see the knot of 46 DNA chromosomes jut as they were before.
- See yourself backing out of the cell nucleus.
- See yourself pulling back out of the cell, back into the tissue of your lungs, out of your body, and back into the present where you sit with your hands interlaced.
- You know that you can come back to look at your DNA at any time.
- Take two or three deep breaths. Slowly open your eyes.

Now repeat the exercise with you reading the visualization to your companion. After you've both completed the exercise, discuss with your companion what each of you experienced. Describe your feelings as you saw your genius in action.

After completing this exercise several times, you may experience a greater sense of self-worth, increased confidence and a natural feeling of trusting your actions and abilities. You may feel this because you are getting in touch with the true encoding of your natural genius — your DNA.

To download the Visualization as an audio file, go to this website address: http://geniuscoaching.net/unlockyourgenius.htm

CHAPTER 7

Specialize to Soar

Once discovered, genius needs to be applied. If you don't apply your genius abilities right now, don't worry; you're not alone. In fact, you're a member of one of the largest clubs on earth — "Unrealized Geniuses of the World."

The marketplace is the engine for stimulating, promoting and rewarding genius. Yet 99 percent of the genius in the world never reaches the marketplace. One reason for this might be that you often have to create your own opportunities.

Create Your Own Opportunities

Progressive corporations provide an excellent arena for developing personal skills. The consistent demand to step up, to do things faster and more effectively, can create exactly the challenge you need to dive into your genius. Remember, genius sometimes doesn't show itself until challenged.

Instead of chafing against corporate structures, make the most of the openings that do exist. Business makes you interact with people that you usually wouldn't get along with, requiring you to do things that you would never think of doing. This stretch can be ideal for applying your genius abilities in a specialized area.

You can't wait for a corporation to give you the opportunity to specialize. You may have to start creating it yourself. Here are some hints on how to do so:

- Become the opposite of what you complain about in others. If you dislike the way others delay tasks until the last minute, for example, finish your tasks early.
- If you see a lack of leadership skills in your supervisor, start providing the leadership missing in your area of responsibility.
- Make suggestions to your colleagues and supervisor about how to improve things.
- Think about how you can assist others around you.
- Take tasks off others' hands that don't cause you excess work but helps them.
- If you have an idea, always express it.

What do you have to lose? If your ideas and new actions are dismissed, you're still expressing your exceptional talent. Go for your expression of genius and don't worry about acceptance. At the very least, you will begin enjoying your work more.

Specialize for Unlimited Growth

Geniuses generally have to create their own connection between their genius abilities and the marketplace. Don't worry about doing it. The marketplace won't dull your genius or corrupt it. The marketplace will help you sharpen and refine your genius. To gain the full benefit, you have to be willing to discover and develop a specific specialty.

Every person has a set of unique genius abilities, which sometimes can be expressed in more than one profession. Leonardo da Vinci, for instance, expressed his genius in eight professions as a painter, anatomist, geometer, sculptor, architect, musician, engineer, and scientist. Having to start with one, he started with drawing at age 14 as an apprentice to the painter Andrea del Verrocchio. His ability to visualize and express the complexity of a form in his drawings showed itself later as the medium he used to express his genius in other fields. You have to put down roots to know where to specialize in your genius area, so you gain a feeling of excellence and being in demand for your talent.

Many people squander their genius because they are afraid to specialize. They don't want to feel trapped. They are good at so many things that they just want to float from one talent to another and back again without ever committing themselves. However, talent is not exactly the same as genius. Genius is the talent or set of abilities that brings you deep satisfaction and financial success only when realized and intentionally focused in one professional area.

A mother recently came to Genius Coaching with a 15 year-old daughter, Sarah, who was bored with the gifted program at school. A straight-A student, Sarah also excelled in music, dance and theater. You might think this girl would be the last person on earth to need coaching, but the girl's divorced mother knew otherwise. Sarah's father had similar capabilities. Although he was very smart, he was never clear about his genius. He never settled on any one area, so he'd struggled all his life. The man became alcoholic, and this led to the divorce. The mother feared her daughter might follow in the father's footsteps. In effect, she feared her daughter's genius may destroy her, thinking it was the same force that had destroyed her husband.

However, genius was not the father's problem. The opposite was true. Despite being extremely smart, he never knew how his skills could work together or how to apply them. He never felt the self-esteem that comes from owning and living his genius.

Genius is not flaky. Genius is committed. Genius is on fire. You don't have to tell your genius to go forward. Your genius tells you to go with it and own it.

Don't be afraid of entering a specific area. Specialization won't limit you. Many people wrongly think they can go big if they apply their skills to anything that comes along. The truth is that you can only go big if you commit and focus, if you jump in all the way. Once you discover the high performance of specialization, you can later apply that experience and understanding to any area that attracts you. Once you cross the threshold of genius, you will never go back to jumping from one idea to the next.

After working with us for several months, Sarah realized her unique genius abilities were in the arts — acting, music, and painting — as well as the complex world of the law. She decided to pursue entertainment law as a career path. Her sharp mind was challenged by the complexity of the law, and she could relate to her future clients because she was a passionate actor herself. Her fear of not picking the right career was gone. She felt a self-confidence and excitement that she'd never felt before.

Start With Being Curious

Specialists start as generalists. You can't specialize in anything if you don't have a field to explore. There are more work opportunities in life than you can possibly imagine. You may feel drawn to a career in the law, for example, but that's only the beginning. To see the scope of your options, search Google or Yahoo for the term "lawyer" (our own recent search yielded 117 million results). Given many different types of lawyers, each specialty brings you in contact with different kinds of people and distinct challenges.

Let's say you're interested in science as well as the law. You may want to practice law as it relates to energy. From there, you may feel especially drawn to the alternative energy industry. You may choose to work on the corporate side, on the government side, or for a relevant non-profit organization. Or you may be a movie buff and opt for entertainment law, which has just as many, if not more, varieties. Every specialty works this way. There is no end to the depths of the niches you can explore, but you'll never find out where your genius really lives unless you get started hunting it down.

Look at your genius abilities. Study your answers from Chapters 1 and 2. Look at all the areas where you perform exceptionally well. What topics stimulate your brilliance? Is it art, law, writing, or business, or a combination of all? Look at the environment in which you most excel. How do you communicate best with others? What communication do you need from others to perform at your best? Do you work better in large teams or on your own? Do you like to manage or be the person who executes? Do you excel with a billion-dollar project, or is a smaller project the perfect challenge for you right now? Look at your life experiences. What have you mastered? What insights can you apply? How can you leverage your talents and interests? If you love to play piano, why take tennis lessons? Do what you love first, yet see the bigger picture. Genius is about living a bigger life.

Ask yourself, "What makes me tick? What is really true about me, and what are just unexamined assumptions? Who am I? And what do I want?" Nothing confuses people more than these questions, so take your time and answer from the heart.

Don't stop there. Discover more of your hidden genius abilities by doing things differently, even everyday things. Change your routine. Eat different foods. Drive home by a different route. For your vacation, visit somewhere new, perhaps abroad, but don't take the tame guided tour. Get a fresh perspective. Explore a new place and you'll explore yourself as well. New actions stimulate new thoughts and new realizations.

Children are great at this. Some friends visiting my house recently brought their four year-old boy with them. He came into my office, so I asked him if he wanted to work on my computer with me. He had no idea what I was talking about, but he said, "Yes." Like children, we have to be ready to say "yes" to new experiences.

Most people mistakenly believe that thoughts lead to action. They are waiting to think and feel something new and then act upon it. They are waiting to be struck by lightening. If that happens, great, but don't wait too long. If you're still hearing that voice inside telling you there must be something more, you've waited long enough.

How Actions Open Big Opportunities

Nothing stimulates genius like action, so don't hold back. Don't wait for all the ducks to line up. They never stay in line anyway, do they? Take action now and adjust as you go. Each time you act you'll move closer and closer to your bull's eye. If you feel like a fish out of water, flop around some. You might fall right into the water you've been looking for. Flopping is a lot better than doing nothing at all.

Did you realize that on a cross-country flight, your plane is off-course 97 percent of the time? The on-board computer constantly has to adjust in the air. Geniuses have to do the same thing. First you have to take off, then choose a direction, set a course, and adjust as you go along. Before you know it, the miles will be passing beneath you, and you'll be landing somewhere brand new. Now that's a journey worth taking.

My own personal struggles at school prove the point.

I had a ridiculously low perception of my own abilities, yet I also had a hunger to do work I liked. In university, I studied Japanese culture, which interested me, but I couldn't see myself making any money with it. I quit and started exploring the marketplace. I had no career path, so I tried many different jobs to see what I liked. I worked in a company that provided industrial laundry services. I worked as a secretary somewhere else.

Finally, I found the job as an account manager at the ad agency. I liked being around creative people. I enjoyed talking to clients on the phone, which was a big part of the job. My challenge — to manage marketing projects involving clients and internal departments — brought out my talent to coordinate complex projects and make everyone win.

Everything I did all day involved communication, which surprised me. I would never have thought that I was any good at communicating. In school I'd always felt like a misfit, which made communication difficult. Only through curiosity and action, through trial and error, did I arrive at this well-paying agency job. For the first time in my working life, I was excited in every way. I was happy.

I went on to better and better jobs in entirely different industries, but this first truly enjoyable and successful experience opened me to seeing that I could find success in the business world. This is my story. What about you?

Geniuses need to have the guts not to be perfect. Don't worry if you make mistakes. Don't take them personally; learn from them. Successful people make more mistakes than the average person, not fewer. They are always taking risks, stretching themselves, always moving beyond what they have known and experienced so far.

Think of the movies. A scene may be re-shot as many as 50 times. When the director calls for another take, what if the star felt like a failure and quit the movie? Most actors don't do that. They see multiple takes as part of the process of making movies. Geniuses likewise need to see that refinement is part of the process of being a genius.

This doesn't mean you should keep on going with a given pursuit no matter what. If something really isn't clicking for you, be real about it. Genius has an inner knowing that tells you whether or not you're on the right track. There has to be progress. If you're still not making progress after a solid effort, it's time to try something different. Your vision may be compelling, but don't settle for a great idea that doesn't work in real life. If you know inside there's something better waiting for you, pursue it.

Your True Dynamic Nature is Your Wild Card in Today's Market

Genius takes its cue from your DNA. Many people perceive DNA to be a fixed map of who you are, but this is not true. The DNA sends out commands, but it also receives feedback. Your DNA always is affected by your cellular metabolism, which is never static. DNA continually responds to its environment while it's affecting it.

We need to allow our natural genius to be just as dynamic. The world stays in constant flux. The marketplace is always evolving. Technology changes business behavior every day. Global conditions impact local decisions. You need your genius to keep up with all of the changes, and you know what? Your genius loves it. Your personality might struggle with change, but your genius thrives on it.

Be open to discovering even more of your genius abilities in the most unlikely places. This openness will free you to seize the best opportunity that presents itself.

Alicia was operating two businesses simultaneously. She had a massage practice and a house cleaning business. She was barely able to pay her monthly bills, yet she felt stuck with both businesses. Before emigrating to the U.S. from Caracas, Venezuela, Alicia had developed a large business in the healing and personal growth called rebirthing. Now faced with a real need to be profitable, rather than restart that practice here, she decided to focus on just one business. She applied her business skills to house cleaning.

House cleaning may not sound as promising or fulfilling as rebirthing or massage, but Alicia saw that her cleaning business was more scalable. She could grow it larger, make more money doing it, and enjoy more freedom with it, which is what she's done.

Today, Alicia has a six-figure cleaning business based on the people and business skills she developed from her holistic health work. She doesn't do any of the cleaning herself. She trains and manages employees as she sells her firm's services. While massage had looked like more fun than cleaning, it would never have given her the best opportunity to apply her real abilities — communication, sales, and business management.

Genius never settles down. Genius doesn't get married to a particular job or business and fall into a routine existence. Genius is always ready for the next step. If you follow your genius, it will always take you to new things.

An example is the career path of T. Harv Eker, who wrote *Secrets of the Millionaire Mind.* In addition to being a marketing genius, he holds seminars in his area of expertise while continually responding to his clients' needs. His first seminar focused on Money, Mind and Spirit. His audience responded well, but he learned that many of them lacked a clear direction in their lives for applying what he was teaching. So, his next seminar was on life directions. He learned that many people in that seminar were entrepreneurs struggling to market themselves. So, his next seminar was the Entrepreneur Boot Camp. By constantly responding to his audiences' needs, Eker has built his company into one of the largest personal development organizations in the U.S.

Don't confuse your starting point with your destination. Once you get your genius going, there is no limit to expanding it. Take your set of genius abilities and think about where you can apply them best. You will be amazed at how fast you can go far beyond the destination. There is no limit to what you can create.

Live your natural genius full out; you can't lose by doing so.

CHAPTER 8

Stop De-Genius-izing Yourself

Now that you are discovering your natural genius, there is really no controlling what will come up in you. You will experience great excitement and excellent ideas. You will also hear directly from the voices that have stopped you in the past, voices that are self-critical and harsh, voices that come from experiences in the past.

I still sometimes hear a voice telling me, "You are weird. You will never really be able to connect to others. People will never like you and never buy from you." This voice came from my past experience in the village where I grew up and at school where I felt like an alien, an outsider. We call these voices your "inner terrorist."

Your inner terrorist is always on the job, poised and ready to keep you fully informed of everything that's wrong with you. Usually the evaluation is based on made-up stuff and lies. Thanks to this tireless critic, you're stopped from feeling too good about yourself or enjoying your abilities too much. In fact, you often can't get into the present moment at all because your mind is absorbed in the past or the future.

A steady stream of negative self-talk is the curse of past experiences and internalized norms from early experiences being expressed in our bodies. Please realize that your inner terrorist is *not* you and has nothing to do with the reality you live in now.

My successes have outgrown my early experiences at school. My thinking should have caught up with reality a long time ago, but the old voices still speak up loudly, especially when I'm tired, when I try out something new, or when someone doubts my actions.

In those moments, I hear inside, "You will always be confined to your own world, and you will never be able to reach anyone with who you really are. Nothing you do will ever be enough because you just don't fit in." The German culture of my youth speaks to me in those moments. Being perfect and not making mistakes is important in Germany. I like the American approach far better; people here are encouraged to explore new things, and making a mistake only becomes an issue if you make the same one over and over again. Although I've known for a long time that perfectionism stifles me, the German voices tell me, "Never step out before you know you can do it perfectly," or after doing something new, "You should have been much better prepared."

Lucky for me, I now know that these voices come from the past. They have nothing to do with my present reality and I can honestly call them *lies.*

I now know that all my actions cause effects. Every time I talk to someone about their genius, they start to think. Some are so inspired that they call later to thank me for the insights. Others decide to explore their genius and start coaching with me. Some dismiss the conversation right away and move to the next topic. I don't know who will respond or how, but as long as I keep talking, people do respond. The voice that said, "You can never connect to people" is one of the biggest lies I ever told myself.

The Inner Terrorist in Action

The excellent movie *Good Will Hunting* offers a clear, if extreme, example of this. The character played by Matt Damon is a mathematical genius with a photographic memory for incredible information recall. He can quote complex economics books by heart, but he's working as a construction laborer and janitor. Why? He was raised by an alcoholic, abusive father who gave him the impression that he was not good at anything. Instead of seeing his genius and pursuing success using his extraordinary skill set, he gets into bar fights and trouble with the law. He applies his brilliance to formulating preposterous legal defenses for himself that ultimately get him into even more trouble.

Good Will Hunting may present an exaggerated case, but to one degree or another, we have all been affected by inner criticism, and never for the better. In fact, this drama of denying our destructive self-talk and embracing our true potential is the underlying story of virtually every popular character-based movie or novel.

Most of us have heard some good things from the people in our lives, but when it comes to genius, we've heard next to nothing or else nothing at all. Some of us have been fortunate enough to have one teacher or one relative who deeply appreciated our abilities, who invited us to put our passion into action. Even if we were lucky enough to have such people around us, we no doubt had others who were not nearly as generous when it came to supporting the expression of our personal genius.

Consequently, when we start to put our genius in action, we often hear an uproar of objection from all those who never had any inkling of what it means to manifest their own genius. We hear fears and doubts and warnings and rejections.

Sadly, the smarter you were in youth, the more of this negation you likely absorbed, simply because you were better at processing information. A good learner often learned a lot of nonsense. So, the inner criticism you hear shouldn't dissuade you from a sense of your genius; it should confirm it. It's a mark of your ability to take in the world around you. In the case of the inner terrorist, you simply ingested the wrong stuff.

Your self-criticism is not real. It's the accumulation of limitations you've learned from others. The more we listen and accept those lies, the wider the gap grows between reality and our negating assumptions about ourselves. Self-talk will even block us from receiving compliments from people that would help us know how great we truly are. That's because the negative messages about us got inside first.

All of us at one time or another have learned from the wrong people. Most of us have received plenty of criticism, not to mention ignorant or bad advice. And let's face it: our parents likely are the dominant source. This doesn't usually mean they wanted to harm us (yet in some cases they did). Our parents may have thought they were protecting us by telling us to aim low, play it safe, think small, or else think big but just don't act on it. These are some of the messages of limitation we've internalized along the way.

People, particularly parents, want you to be like them or how they would like to be. This secures them in their status quo, no matter how unfulfilling it may be. If our parents have been quite fulfilled, the pressure to become "them" can be even stronger. However, being your parents will never be fulfilling to you. You must be you. The consequence is that you need to free yourself from your inner terrorist.

Liberation can't be achieved through negotiation. You can't negotiate with a terrorist, whose goals are not even remotely similar to your goals, your joy or your best interests. In fact, if you try to negotiate with your inner terrorist, the effort only strengthens those negative voices. They are absolutely ruthless about refusing to give you any credibility for being a natural genius. In turn, you must be ruthless about stopping your inner critic. You can't make peace with the inner terrorist because it doesn't want peace. You can't ignore the inner terrorist because it's operating in the background anyway. Most importantly: you can't fight it head-on because such a fight is like pouring oil onto a burning fire. Your only option is to call a lie a lie. You must starve the inner terrorist out of existence.

Take a Stand for Your Genius

Here is where the genius trait of a passion for reality proves helpful. You know your genius abilities; you have identified your ideal playground or specialty to best apply your genius; and you get great results. Producing great results is the best weapon against your inner terrorist. Your inner terrorist thrives on smallness. The bigger you play, the faster your inner terrorist will be starved out of existence.

I've experienced over and over again that when I talk to people with my genius in full action, I always get a certain percentage of new clients, which means I connect. The more I talk, the more clients I get. My new reality replaces the voice from the past that said, "You will never connect because you are weird and an outsider." The more I live my natural genius, the more all of my old voices lose their power.

Otto experienced something different when he confronted his inner terrorist.

"I knew that my genius was all my exceptional abilities combined — my 17 years in teaching plus my scientific knowledge of the human body from my master's in biology and chemistry along with my ability to see the genius in others. I'd begun as a learning consultant for children and became successful in less than a year. My unique combination of genius abilities helped me design a 10-step program that hadn't existed before, helping children keep up in the very competitive German school system. Parents were thrilled since many of them feared their children wouldn't qualify for the highest level in German schools and consequently wouldn't have a strong academic career. For the first time in my life, I was successful with something that mattered to me. All the loud voices from my wife, friends and family that said, 'You are a failure,' finally faded away."

Such success is what stopping the inner terrorist is all about. Success won't eliminate fear. Fear can be useful, for it stops us from doing stupid things that could hurt us, but low self-esteem will blow your fears out of proportion.

Every human being has an innate desire to create. Unfortunately, most of us do not have a cheerleader in our heads saying, "Yes, you are great, keep going, don't stop!" The good news is that we can create people in our lives who remind us of our natural genius, who hold us accountable to the reality of our genius, people who encourage us when our voices do not, people who dare to say these negative voices are lies.

Put a paper and crayons in front of a two year-old and a four year-old; they are going to start drawing. Immerse these children in a foreign country; they will begin learning the new language. Learning, growing, creating and expressing are innate qualities of human beings. However, as an adult, there are few people who will tell you that you have the same capacity for expansion as a child. There are no systems in place that support you to experience yourself in this way. Therefore, we need to be loud about our genius, and we need to get loud support from others to help us go beyond the lies.

The inner critic can suppress the innocence, playfulness, curiosity and exploration that help us identify our genius abilities. This terrorist can stop every genius in their tracks. That's why it's vital to know how to stop it. We need to take a stand for our natural genius and set clear boundaries to stop the inner terrorist.

Three Steps to Stopping Your Inner Terrorist

To help you stop your inner terrorist, use the following three steps.

1. Notice.
2. Set Boundaries.
3. Replace.

Step 1
Notice: Welcome the Ghosts of the Past

The first step in silencing your negative voices is to notice them. Most self-talk is really easy to identify once you've given it the right name. That's because this stuff is absurdly repetitive. In fact, such self-talk is the furthest thing from genius. There's nothing original, inspired or fresh about it. Our inner terrorist just repeats the same piece of negation you've played over in your head thousands of times.

You probably wouldn't tolerate that kind of mind-numbing monotony under any other circumstances. For some reason, we make a special accommodation in our lives for negation. This probably has something to do with our primitive survival instinct, which suggests that we cannot afford to take our eyes off any of our faults — real or imagined — lest we pay a terrible price. Actually, we're paying the price every second of every day by listening to our inner terrorist. We pay in the loss of our confidence, our excitement, and our inspiration to grow.

There's biology behind this repetition as well. Your self-criticism uses the same nerve connections as your brain's language center. Those same circuits fire over and over again. The more you allow your negative voices to reign, the more natural it is for you to believe what they say is true. In this way, the gap between what is real and what you think is real grows wider and wider.

Don't be afraid to be aware of your self-talk. Most likely any negative voice about you or anyone else comes from your inner terrorist. and it's a lie. Don't be afraid of conjuring up ghosts that might otherwise leave you alone. If you're not aware that this negation of your value is happening, you can't do much about it. While what you're hearing isn't real, the effect of it certainly can be. When you let the voices in your head talk you out of acknowledging your genius and keep you from exploring the opportunities that genius opens up, that is tragically real.

Be alert. Take note of any negative voice in you. Do so without any judgment or criticism of yourself. Simply be aware. Notice it. There are physical sources for your self-criticism. Now that you understand this, you no longer can be a victim of this negation. So there's really no point in beating yourself up about it. This is the end of your self-inflicted wounds.

Step 2
Set Boundaries: Say "No"

Once you recognize when your inner terrorist is in action, you have to distance yourself from it by setting boundaries. This is a physical activity. You need courage and determination to call a lie a lie. You have to say "no" to the limitations of those negative voices. Saying "no" is the most powerful way of setting boundaries known to man. Children love to learn and apply this word because it halts the conversation and turns all eyes on them.

"No" also is the one word that helps you keep your focus. You have to say "no" to a lot of things before you can say a clear "yes" to the one thing you really want to do. There are millions of professions and business opportunities out there, but once you find your natural genius and where you can live it best, you will need to say no to all of the other options. The same happens with your genius. Once you decide to accept the reality that there is a genius in you at all times, that your unique set of genius abilities provides a tremendous value to others, you now have to say "no" to everything that is contrary. For example, if an inner voice dismisses your ideas or calls your actions slow, inappropriate or insignificant, the "no" will help you draw the boundary and stay on track with your natural genius.

For example, our client Marcia is a realtor. While building her realty business, she works as a registered nurse, a field where she's very experienced. When she comes in for coaching sessions, she has a clear idea where she wants to take her business, how many people she wants working for her, how much revenue she wants to earn.

In her day-to-day living, however, Marcia can't hold her focus. Her self-criticism is too loud. Everything seems overwhelming to her. She's smothered in feelings of failure. She has a doomsday view of her real estate business, and despite 20 years of success in the medical field, she's fearful of losing her nursing job, as well! That's how out of touch with reality our inner critic can make us.

Marcia's negative voices tell her that she's going to fail in real estate, be fired from nursing, and end up living on the street. These loud voices blot out the compliments she receives for her work. When her nursing supervisor praises how she handles a difficult patient, she doesn't hear it. When she closes a deal on a house, she needs to stop for a while before she can allow herself to go for the next one.

How could such an able and industrious person as Marcia have such a low opinion of herself? In her case, it comes straight from her mother. As a little girl growing up, Marcia's mother frequently would tell her she was never going to add up to anything. Granted, Marcia is way too talented and motivated to fulfill this dark prophecy from her mother, but she hasn't been able to free herself of it entirely, either.

After setting a boundary for her inner critic over and over again, she was able to shift this self-defeating pattern of thinking. The negative voice of her mother in her head finally stopped for good.

In less than a year of coaching, Marcia was succeeding so well in her real estate business that she stopped nursing and transitioned to real estate completely. By early spring of the next year, she already had closings scheduled that would bring her more income than she had ever before earned in her entire life.

Step 3
Replace: Your Genius Reality

Once you identify your inner critic and say "no" to it, you have to replace the old message with the truth.

When Marcia did not have the results she wanted in her real estate business and couldn't prove her terrorist wrong yet, she needed to replace her mother's message that she would never amount to anything. She needed contradictory input. She had to start paying attention to all the great feedback she received from her colleagues in nursing and from all of her clients in real estate. After all, Marcia told herself, her mother was never an expert on nursing or real estate, so why should her mother have the last word?

Marcia had to change who she trusted for guidance. She had to acknowledge that a sincere compliment from her supervisor at work was much more significant in the here and now than something negative a parent said to her thirty years ago. She had to recognize the evidence of her own bank account and lifestyle. She had to see that it was now way too late for her to "never amount to anything." She already had been successful for a long time, and she was just beginning.

Ultimately, Marcia had to acknowledge the most important information of all — the feeling about herself that comes from her own genius abilities encoded in her DNA. She had to replace the learned with the innate.

What we are taught may not be who we are. The inner terrorist never says how you are great, successful, or worthy. It just repeats all the negative messages you were taught. Your job is telling yourself who you are and what you are capable of doing. Positive self-talk does not come naturally, but you have to exercise your own powers of communication to replace the negative voices with what is truly real.

An Example

Remember to apply all three steps in sequence: *Notice. Set boundaries. Replace.*

Your inner terrorist says you are not important. Instead of just suppressing this voice and feeling down for no reason, identify and notice this negative voice.

Immediately say "no" to the voice. Set the necessary boundary and announce to yourself that you have no space for such criticism and lies. But don't stop there.

Give yourself a new direction right away. For example, you now need to declare, "I make a huge difference with my unique genius abilities," or, "I am valuable."

By replacing your negative self-talk with reality, you are doing more than arguing with some relative. You are physically re-educating your brain to use different nerve connections to break the endless loop of self-negation. Clearly and confidently, you are giving yourself credit for being a natural genius. You are passionate, excited, curious, and open, and ready to live the life you always wanted to live right now.

Download your free report: *The 19 Best Ways to Stop Your Inner Terrorist*
http://geniuscoaching.net/stopyourterrorist.htm

CHAPTER 9

Your Genius: The Secret Weapon for Prosperity

Your genius will take you places you've never gone before. Do not be alarmed.

This is especially true when it comes to money. If you have never earned the kind of money you really wanted to earn, or if you've made good money but never really enjoyed what you did for a living, then it's time you tapped into the prosperity of your genius. It's time for you to take advantage of the serendipity of your natural genius.

Once you identify your genius abilities and apply them where they fit best, you easily stick out in the marketplace. Your unique offering gives a certain group of people exactly what they want. You earn high fees as an expert. Your genius and expertise continuously improves, which causes your fees to rise, so your profits grow as you grow. The amount of money you earn and the manner in which you earn it align with your natural genius. You love what you do, and you are being paid well for doing it.

Does this sound too good to be true? Well, this is the life you create when you go with your natural genius. *Genius is the shortcut to prosperity* because the market rewards specialization with higher compensation. Also, when you love what you do, people feel it and want to be around you. You stand out from your competitors, which enables you to attract the kind of clients and working conditions you desire.

You've probably heard stories to the contrary that genius and prosperity are somehow two separate matters. Indeed, some extraordinary individuals have managed to do great things and were not compensated for them. It's tough to accomplish, but not impossible.

Take the Dutch painter Vincent Van Gogh (1853 - 1890). Three of his paintings are on the list of 10 most expensive paintings, and one of his paintings was sold for $82,500,000. While he was alive, however, Van Gogh sold only one painting. He was never prosperous, and his genius went unrecognized until long after he'd passed away.

One of the most famous painters of the age, Gauguin, was a friend of Van Gogh, that is, until Van Gogh chased him away with an open razor. Van Gogh was mentally unstable. There were reasons for his lack of sales that had nothing to do with his genius.

Extraordinary people attract attention, but often of the most ignorant kind. Shallow gossip tends to mask the facts and reinforce whatever common prejudice already exists. Small wonder that in a world promoting the idea that wealth is only for the few and very difficult to obtain, stories of unrewarded talent are the ones we hear most often.

In this way the general public has been "dumbed down" and encouraged to maintain a split mind about money and genius. And yet the evidence to the contrary is everywhere — Thomas Edison, Henry Ford, Walt Disney, Oprah Winfrey, Sam Walton. They all have plenty of money to show for their efforts.

Consider the case of 2007 Oscar winner Martin Scorsese, whose Italian-American parents worked low jobs in New York's Garment District. A sickly child, he spent much of his time stuck at home with asthma, at which time he developed his passion for film. As an adult, he's not only made great movies, he's also made great money.

What about "The King" himself, Elvis Presley, who changed the culture with the sway of his hips? His estate is still worth many millions of dollars. What about the geniuses of business, the foremost being Bill Gates, one of the wealthiest men in the world, or Warren Buffett, the greatest investor of our time? If they can grow prosperous from their genius, you can too. You may not become a national icon, but you will definitely become known in your field of expertise. How far do you want to go?

Yes, there have been brilliant people who were never duly rewarded for their talents. This was in spite of their abilities, not because of them. In reality, genius and money go hand in hand. Making money won't ruin your innate talents; it will only heighten them and give you greater comfort and confidence to manifest yourself more fully.

No Matter Where, Your Genius is Your Biggest Money Maker

Genius is not a career path. Genius is the passion for excellence that burns inside you. If you follow that passion, your genius will lead you to larger and larger opportunities, so you can't stay locked into one predetermined plan.

When Otto and I moved to the United States, we did so because we believed a greater life was awaiting us here. We felt excited about the opportunities to expand ourselves, yet we did not have every aspect of the transition planned out perfectly.

In fact, when we arrived, we'd imagined restarting our business as learning consultants on this side of the Atlantic. Our business did not catch on as fast as we would have liked. Since we had bills to pay, we were both forced to make other arrangements. Worry about how to make ends meet doesn't support the innovative playfulness of genius.

My first job in the U.S. was as a business manager at the Scottsdale Artists' School in Arizona. I was drawn by the creative atmosphere more than the money. The job paid only $22,000 a year to start. At the time, this seemed perfect because I was facing a completely new culture. Everyone wore similar fashions and lived in comparable circumstances to what I'd known in Germany, but when I looked closer, nothing was the same.

Americans thought and felt differently about pretty much everything — boyfriends, children, marriage, career, friends, retirement, vacations, recycling, cars, job security, health insurance, and lots more. I was constantly translating in my head from German, not just the language, but the entire environment. One of my biggest challenges was that what I had done so successfully in Germany seemed not to match anything in the U.S. I'd been an account manager for an ad agency, but it was called "Kontakter" in Germany, and I didn't know how to translate that to anything in the U.S.

Still, I didn't stay put. Within two years, I moved to a corporation as an administrative assistant for a higher salary of $33,500. Although I enjoyed earning more money, I felt frustrated and bored with the work I was doing. I'd felt the same with every job I started. The work was fascinating and exiting to me for two weeks, then the routine kicked in. Since boredom is one of my worst enemies, I started to have nightmares. My doctor wanted to put me on high blood pressure medication. Far worse than being bored, I hadn't found a playground for my genius abilities to express themselves. I'd never been great at grammar and spelling and just following instructions without carrying responsibility, so working as an administrative assistant was a nightmare to me.

While I was in a new country and didn't know the language or culture, my advantage was that I knew my genius abilities. I was very clear about the fact that I wasn't applying my genius as an administrative assistant. So I kept looking. I read tons of job descriptions on Monster.com and kept going to interviews.

After four months in an administrative support job, I applied for a new position in the company called "Associate Account Service Coordinator." The job description indicated that I'd be able to apply my communication skills to create order when everything seemed in chaos. I landed the job and received a raise to $42,000.

I felt more at home in the new job. I could express more of myself, and it showed to everyone around me. The serendipity of genius started to kick in. Three months after I started in the new job, a senior account services person left. We were working on a $4.5 million account, the fourth-largest account in our firm. The sales team had just won this client from our competitor. At a previous meeting, I'd made a favorable impression on that client, so they requested me as their new account service coordinator, which meant a raise to $54,000 annually. After just four months in the new post, I was thrown into a more challenging position. I felt afraid, but my natural genius came out in full swing.

Please note that no one in the company had ever followed the route I'd taken, from strictly administrative work into account management. I was breaking new ground. I soon became a senior account manager earning $64,000 with a bonus worth $20,000. When I left the company to join Genius Coaching, the company offered me a position with an earning potential in the low six figures!

Remember that I'd started at $22,000. Only seven years, later I was offered a position worth five times that amount. How did I make such exponential progress? I did it not by following a career path, but by never compromising on my genius abilities. I knew how it felt to express my genius, and I didn't want to settle for less.

If I'd been hung up on a career path, I may never have started at the Scottsdale Artists' School. I needed that experience to acclimate to American culture, to sharpen my English and prepare for the next phase. If I'd begun in the corporate climate, which is much less forgiving, I might have been stopped before I started. Once there, I got what I needed and moved on. I never created a comfort zone in which I knew every detail of any job, so I could do it in my sleep. Genius doesn't settle down. Genius needs new stimulation and opportunities to expand. Each time I needed a door opened for me, I started looking and found it. This paid off handsomely in both job satisfaction and money!

Easy Money

Genius money is easy money. This is a natural byproduct of living your genius abilities full out. You make big things happen without even trying, it seems. But it's not enough for you to experience your genius by yourself. You also have to take off your mask, stop playing dumb and accept the recognition of others.

Too many people filter out praise. They are nearly as guarded about compliments as they are about insults. When a client or a colleague says, "You did a great job," do you really take that in, or do you qualify it? Do you tell yourself in one way or another: "He doesn't really mean it?" Or perhaps: "He doesn't know what he's talking about." If you cannot accept praise for your genius, how can you welcome prosperity?

One way to find out if praise is sincere is to see if money accompanies the nice words. In the marketplace, money is the fundamental acknowledgement of good work. If people say they love your work but don't want to pay you for it, they really don't value what you do enough. On the other hand, if they pay you what you ask and more, you can be very sure they appreciate your work.

However, prosperity is more than money. Real prosperity includes social recognition, personal satisfaction, and appreciation of your skills in non-monetary forms. However, true prosperity rarely exists without money.

When the money starts flowing, don't worry. Money will not distract you from your genius. Money will only nourish and inspire you to manifest your genius in greater ways, which in turn will lead to more money. In fact, you may generate money so spontaneously and without apparent effort that you fail to give yourself proper credit for it.

Many of us don't receive full credit for our own creation simply because it doesn't come in the way we expect. Marc is a writer who aspired to a literary career, which can be a long and difficult process. To support himself, he created a business writing marketing materials and non-fiction books for others.

Marc was so focused on trying to launch his literary career that he regularly missed his genius for his business. He'd written for virtually every kind of audience imaginable, from mechanical engineers to teenage girls. He'd created extremely lucrative opportunities for himself, but he failed to fully appreciate them.

In his second year of business, Marc was approached about writing and supervising the writing, of several whitepapers that would present a brand new line of products to the marketplace on behalf of a Fortune 100 company. He realized it was a big project, but he was uncertain how much to charge for his services. He felt nervous about asking for too much and losing the project. The client solved this by volunteering that they could pay no more than $20,000 dollars for the project. This sum was about four times higher than what he'd thought to request. The project provided nearly half of the total money he earned that year. His genius for business showed up for the first time. Over the next few years, Marc learned to combine his genius for writing with his genius for business. His income doubled!

Your Natural Genius is Worth Millions

Here is where the inner game of prosperity comes into play. We have to let ourselves *feel* the value of what we do. It isn't an ego trip to feel that you are worthy of prosperity. Ego is when you really don't feel the value of who you are, and you are constantly trying to keep up an image. You might achieve increased earnings, but you can't really enjoy your creation — only the impression you can make on others.

When someone pays you well for your work, take it personally. Let this soak into your bones. Make the connection that this isn't just a random event; this is who you are. Don't be afraid of getting used to a higher pay scale. If it's really you, no one can take it away from you. The check has your name on it, not someone else's.

You don't have to be perfect to be paid well, but you have to strive for excellence. Perfection is an abstract concept and a "closed system" that has nothing to do with the tangible products and services you might provide. You have to recognize the value your genius creates for other people. You have to go with it.

Let the money expand you. Do something you've never done before with it. Save more. Invest more. Spend more. Give more. Now your natural genius is carrying over into every aspect of your life, and you are in total prosperity mode.

When you set aside the inner debate about whether you are good enough or deserving enough to make more money, that's when your genius kicks into gear and your earnings increase exponentially.

Our client Jill, a master mortgage broker, experienced this first-hand. In 14 months she increased her income from $85,000 a year to $240,000 a year. Just so you get the full picture, as a single mother with four boys ranging in age from 6 to 14 years old. Jill already had a full plate. So how did she nearly triple her income? Not by working harder — she was already maxed out in that department — but by believing in herself, going with her natural genius, and building a team of smart support people around her.

When it comes to real estate financing, Jill is a superior strategist. This aptitude lent itself to real estate investors more than simple homebuyers, since investors have to consider many added factors in determining their best course of action. Jill needed to have the confidence in herself to specialize in the investors' market and know inside that she could build a strong business in the mortgage niche. By recognizing her genius talent and following it, she tapped into more repeat business. After all, investors buy and sell homes far more frequently than your typical homebuyer.

To further focus on her innate abilities, Jill needed support. She had to hire a marketer to promote her and bring in new clients, and a loan processor to do the paper work. These were not areas of genius for her. In fact, these chores were distractions from her genius. By eliminating these distractions, Jill was able to concentrate on being Jill — a wiz at attracting new clients and processing data to develop sound investment strategies. Hiring staff also let her begin leveraging her excellence in new ways — through public speaking and teaching. As if all that was not enough, she has built her own home and purchased four investment properties in the process.

The key for Jill was to stop blocking herself with doubts about whether or not she could do it and just let her genius take over.

What about you?

CHAPTER 10

Genius Leadership: Multiply Your Success

Once you develop a sense for your natural genius, once you know where to apply your unique set of genius abilities, you become happier than ever before. You earn more money than ever before, so you can afford to step up your lifestyle. You may think, "This is all I ever imagined." Your vision may seem fulfilling at first, but you soon see the limits of what you can do on your own. As your vision expands, your genius grows beyond only you. You need other people. First, you need others to delegate all the tasks that are not in your genius area. Second, you need more people to reach more people.

Where would Paul Allen be today if he had stopped at himself? By all accounts, the co-founder of Microsoft was a gifted programmer even in high school. His passion grew so intense that he dropped out of Washington State University to pursue it. He went beyond his solo act by convincing a high school friend, Bill Gates, to drop out of Harvard and join him. For better or worse, that was leadership. Allen allowed his enthusiasm to rub off on another person. He altered the course of both their careers.

Allen again tapped the services of others in 1980 when Microsoft bought the rights to an operating system called QDOS for $50,000. Microsoft used QDOS to win a contract for supplying the operating system of the new IBM Personal Computer, the first PC from which all others were cloned. This DOS operating system became the foundation of Microsoft's remarkable growth. Neither Allen nor Gates had actually written the DOS code themselves. They used the talents of others to fulfill their vision.

Geniuses Are Natural Leaders

Once you discover your genius, you have to be a leader, or else you deny your genius the joy of being shared with others. As a specialist, you are a leading authority. You have a responsibility to be a leader in your field. First, you've led yourself through your own doubts and intimidations. Second, by introducing something new to your clients, you're already leading them. Inevitably, you have the realization that no matter how magnificent your kingdom of one may be, you want to operate on a larger scale.

How do you expand? You enroll good people who can help you to bring about the greater expression of your genius. This can be a startling realization. Suddenly, it's not all about you. Suddenly, your innate talents demand the excellence of others.

Don't worry! You don't necessarily have to run out and read all the latest books about leadership and become an expert in that field. Instead, you have to open your mind to bringing in other people who can assist you. Rather than a knock on your own abilities; it's a confirmation of them. You've outgrown merely being self-employed. You now need a team to execute your plan. Congratulations!

Demand Genius Performance

Just as your genius doesn't show up in any random arena, you can't haphazardly build your team with anyone who answers a help wanted ad. You must be selective about those who work with you. The right people will be drawn to you and how you operate. You care about excellence, so bring in other people who care about it. Don't be afraid to ask them directly, "Can you provide excellence in this position?" Look them in the eye and be aware of their body language. You'll very quickly know where they stand.

Excellence knows excellence. You will recognize each other. To do this, though, you can't be ambivalent about your own business. To stir the standard of excellence in others, you must be aware and committed to excellence in yourself.

Fred owns a marketing and communications firm. When a problem arose with an assistant who was new to the business, Fred couldn't quite pinpoint what bothered him. He felt impatient with her progress but not just because of her inexperience.

As we discussed with Fred his concerns, he realized that it was her level of engagement that irritated him. She wasn't operating at full speed. She wasn't giving him excellence. Had he ever discussed this with her? Had he ever said to her point blank, "I need your excellence; are you willing to give that?"

The answer was "no," and Fred quickly saw why not. At the time, he was interested in transitioning to a speaking career. He had already started viewing his current business as secondary. Without himself being totally committed to excellence in his business, how could he require excellence from his assistant? Fred experienced that leadership reflects right back on the leader's personal integrity with being a natural genius.

Your own passion for excellence is your most important asset when it comes to leadership. From the start, communicate what you want and what you feel. Let people know how passionate you feel. You'll sense very quickly whether they are buying into your vision. On the other hand, if you are passive or uncertain about your own hunger for excellence, you will never be able to draw out the best from others.

Many people out there can be outstanding members of your team, so don't stop until you find them. As a genius leader, you may be able to work around a lack of experience or some shortcoming in a team member's skill set, but you will never be comfortable with someone who has no appetite for excellence. This must be your bottom line requirement. If a person does not share your passion for the work, that person does not belong on your team. What can be simpler?

Please don't believe that your own abilities as a leader can change this trait in a person. You cannot lead the wrong people. No amount of management skill or knowledge can change this fact. There are some people in whom you can invest yourself and some people you cannot. The sooner you recognize this, the sooner you will focus your energy on the people who can really move your team forward.

Use Your Personal Genius Experience to Show Others the Way

Once you identify the right people for your team, be prepared to go all the way with them. By this we mean, don't give up on them just because some issue might emerge.

Remember, some people have never acted on their hunger for high quality or natural genius, least of all in a professional setting. Your job is to awaken that in them.

Be aware that even the right people often have some baggage. Reflect on your own experience in tapping into your natural genius. No doubt it was not without obstacles. The same is true for your team members.

As a leader, you need to support and strengthen the desire for genius in others. You need to set high standards and make bold requests. Do not accept the lies of the inner terrorist acting up in your team members at any time. You cannot afford sympathy for anything else but genius because it would affect you, and most likely your own negative voices would come up again.

After all, you are only requesting from others what has brought you to success. Sometimes you may have to dig through a few layers of mediocrity before you get to the gold. But you know it's there. Genius is written in your DNA, and it's worth the effort. If you can find your genius talents, so can others. Just as you have found success by living from your genius, you can support others in doing the same.

You're not searching for perfection in these others any more than you are in yourself. Genius has nothing to do with that. Perfection is limited. Perfection has its boundaries. Perfection has an end. Excellence never finishes expressing itself.

Help your team members create clarity around their innate genius abilities, just as you had to do it yourself. Now you are in the business not only of manifesting your own genius, but in stimulating genius into life and daily expression in others.

Don't worry or think that this will take away from who you are. The more excellence you have around you, the more in touch you get with your own.

Hold the Genius Vision and Create the Direction

The more people you bring onto your team, the clearer you must be about what you want to accomplish. Everyone will have their own impressions and opinions, especially if they are enthusiastic participants. Some of these may be of great value, and some may be off the mark. You must remain true to your core vision and personal integrity.

Suggestions are great because they give people a way to be involved. The more definite you are about what you seek to achieve, the more fluid you'll be in fielding suggestions. You can easily discard ideas that don't support your direction. You can just as easily take up those ideas that enhance your mission.

In order to get the right response from your team, you must effectively communicate your vision, not once, but over and over. Be as specific as possible. Don't leave blanks unless you want people to fill in those blanks themselves. That's exactly what we do when reading stories. For example, if a house is mentioned in a story but not described in detail, we automatically furnish the home ourselves. Make certain you tell your story or vision clearly, and don't leave significant sections open to interpretation.

You can't assume your people will understand you, and you can't assume they won't. You may have to go to the furthest extent to be understood. You can't settle for feeling rejection or discomfort. You have to stand for exactly what you feel.

People sense how you embody your natural genius. You have to radiate it and be fully energized by your expertise. Then, when you are communicating with your team, there is more than just talking going on. There's an exchange of energy that's felt physically.

Diversity: Your Guarantee for Success

Treat your team members like the natural geniuses they are inside. Manifesting natural genius has required you to step out beyond existing norms and systems. You didn't rebel. You did not try to change those norms and systems; you simply didn't want to be locked into them. So don't plug your team members into a system that you yourself worked hard to escape. They don't necessarily have to endure all the challenges you endured. Just like each individual and each genius quality, the path taken to find genius is unique for every person. Remember that your ultimate goal is to get your team to perform at their best, and they can't do that if they pay too high of a price for it.

Just as your genius is fundamentally unique and as one-of-a-kind as your fingerprint, so is the natural genius of your team members. Don't attempt to clone yourself into them. The effort is futile. Even if you succeed in inspiring imitation, you'll never get their best that way. Like your own innate abilities, theirs are entirely original and cannot be copied. Instead, stimulate them to bring out their best originality in service to your overall vision. Allow them to find their own way to contribute. You're not sacrificing your natural genius by doing this; you're multiplying it.

Realizing that people are different is probably the biggest challenge all leaders face. George, an extremely accomplished corporate executive, served as chief financial officer (CFO) for a Fortune 100 company. Given his qualifications, he joined an entertainment company of roughly 200 employees. About a year later he took on the job of interim chief executive officer (CEO). While great at what he does, George constantly clashed with his human resources (HR) manager, Nora.

George and Nora were different types of people. He is an analytical perfectionist; she is an emotional communicator. George kept offending her feelings with his abrupt emails. He claimed to have no time to express a standard level of appreciation, but in the end he spent more time struggling with her feelings by not doing so. George also criticized how Nora laid out the company newsletter since it didn't match his own taste in design, again creating much internal strife. George had the power, so the staff sympathized with Nora, which fed the company gossip mill. Every week some new problem came up.

We could focus on each individual issue that arose between these two, but it came down to George needing to develop the flexibility to lead someone entirely different from himself. While outstanding at what he does, he needed to support other exceptional talents to come forth in styles other than his own.

Nora's emotional genius made her a genius at connecting with people. As an HR manager, this is what she is supposed to do. She had an ease with people that he lacked. She needed to be different from him, and he needed to acknowledge it. Once he did, his job as CEO became a lot easier. Not only could George stop struggling with her, he could focus Nora's talents towards advancing his company-wide agenda. Within a few months of this breakthrough, they'd created a lasting genuine respect for each other.

"Unmanageable" People Can Be the Jackpot You Were Seeking

One day George surprised us with a profound insight. "I love being the CEO," he said. "It puts me more in touch with people on all levels." Being the CEO had been the perfect opportunity for several of his dormant genius abilities to reveal themselves. He translated the company vision into daily business requirements that brought the whole company together. By giving the company clear direction, he achieved the best financial results ever in the history of his division.

One of George's genius abilities was bringing out the genius in team members, especially high performers who didn't easily fit into the system. For instance, the parent company in Austria had sent a new creative design director, Larry, to lead the research and development department. Before Larry even started, a rumor flew around that he was an unmanageable loner, creative but crazy, and that he never got along with anyone. A true artist and entrepreneur with outrageous ideas, Larry connected instantly with George, who recognized Larry's excellence immediately. George and Larry's partnership became one of the key reasons for making the American division the most successful ever.

Genius leadership supports passion rather than suppresses it. This sounds obvious, but passion often threatens our sense of control. Passion involves open communication and discussions. Passion often appears chaotic. As geniuses, we've learned to trust the storm of creativity when it is happening inside us. When it's happening in other people, we need to stay just as open and accommodating.

One way to nurture talent is to become curious about it. What are your team members really good at doing? Give them opportunities to show you. Take a keen interest in each person. You've learned to listen to your own natural genius; now listen for the genius of others. You might hear something they are not even aware of themselves. You might open a door for them they never even knew they were seeking. When you start finding genius in other people, you help them recognize it, as well.

Don't be afraid of a team member surpassing you. Everyone is unique, and you're not in competition with your own organization. You want your people to see their own value. Don't try to hide it from them. Build trust by supporting your team to display their excellence fully without any fear of retribution. In some work environments, excellence is a punishable offense. You don't want your place to be one of them. Your trust will free them to show you their weaknesses, too. Knowing they're appreciated for what they do well, they tell you straight out what they are not so good at doing. This can save you a lot of time and trouble. Better to hear the bad news from them than from a customer!

Encourage Uniqueness yet Require Alignment

You are encouraging talent, but you have no time for people to play out their own self-centered agenda. Genius leadership is about creating feelings of community, but there can be no community without agreement on your purpose. Your personal integrity will be the guiding star to build a culture of trust.

Do not insist that everyone agree with you. Disagreements can help you arrive at more real and fully felt agreements. As the leader, you need to require open dialogue. If a team member has a conflict with you, if you do not confront him or her on the issue, the dispute will only get worse. Conflict can be intense. People take disagreement personally. That is no reason to shy away. At the same time as you voice your disagreement, tell them, "I care about you. I want more for you. That's why I do this." And you have to mean it! You have to lead with a pure intention — it's your personal integrity in action.

George faced such a leadership opportunity with Matt, a highly qualified director slated for promotion to a vice president. George kept bottled water for himself, his staff and his visitors in a little refrigerator outside his office in the reception area. Matt kept stopping by to take a bottle or two without permission. Identifying Matt's behavior as passive-aggressive did not ease the confrontation between him and George.

Through executive coaching, both of these high performers voiced their need for mutual respect. Seeing the bigger picture beyond superficial competitiveness over water bottles, they each acknowledged their mutual value to the organization. When Matt was promoted, he received his own little refrigerator loaded with bottled water. Matt soon was nominated as one of three company officers.

Don't Guess, Get Feedback

Now that you have a team around you, use them to find out how good of a job you are doing in leading them. Your perceptions of yourself may be very different from theirs. Get feedback from your team members. You can ask for it personally, or use a third party to gather feedback anonymously, which might garner more frank responses.

We recently conducted an executive leadership survey for Sam, CEO of a fast-growing business. All of his peers and those employees reporting to him directly were surveyed. The responses were overwhelmingly positive. Out of 25 questions, only one response was slightly less than excellent.

This feedback caught Sam completely off guard. He had no idea he was doing such a good job. He questioned the respondents to learn if they were biased, and he had several direct conversations with them. Much to his astonishment, he gained more encouraging and specific comments for his leadership style, which caused him to reflect even more about his "inner game." He wondered, "How do I actually make people want to work for me? What exactly is my leadership style? What are my personal motivators? What exactly is my leadership excellence all about?"

During his entire career, Sam had grown used to constructive criticism or "sandwich-feedback" — some positive comments followed by negative comments concluding with superficial niceties. He'd accumulated hurt feelings and become defensive to all feedback. Could it be that period was over now, that people genuinely recognized his natural genius for leadership? Could it be time to say "good bye" to his false humility and simply accept honest praise as nourishment for this unique ability?

Personal Integrity Turbo-Charges Your Business

All this comes down to the core of *genius leadership* — the personal integrity of the leader. Genius leaders have the courage to face everything and avoid nothing. They communicate directly person-to-person. They care about other people with a true passion for reality. Honesty is a shortcut in business and life, not just a moral value. A trust-based culture is a natural consequence of people interacting on this high level of personal integrity without any gap between intent and behavior.

The Japanese have three terms for a human being — "immature being," "adult," and "being among others." These correspond to Stephen R. Covey's idea in *The 7 Habits of Highly Effective People* that we each need to mature from dependence to independence to interdependence. His son, Stephen H.R. Covey, wrote in *The Speed of Trust* that real trust is based upon integrity, intent, capabilities, and results. Trust leads to greater speed in business and higher profit margins, he writes. "Trust is one of the most powerful forms of motivation and inspiration."

Genius leadership is based entirely on personal integrity as the highest level of human maturity. It's easy and almost natural to follow a leader who is authentic and clear in his or her communication.

CHAPTER 11

Genius Community: The End of Loneliness

Natural genius is not turned on and off.

Natural genius is not something you do.

Natural genius is who and what you are because it is your natural birthright.

We've been brought up in a culture that's extremely confused about genius, a society that doesn't readily acknowledge that genius is for everyone. Rather, our society reserves the term for a very special few — the "Einsteins" among us — while dismissing the rest. Unfortunately, this trickles down to all of us.

If you ask 100 people if they are a genius, 99 will most likely say, "No way, not me." By contrast, we feel that out of 100 people, 100 should say "Yes, I'm a genius, and my unique set of genius abilities is here in this area where I live it every day."

Genius Sustains Genius

You need to make a particular effort to sustain this new way of genius and resist being drawn back into your old existence by all the people that don't feel their genius. You can't do it just by walking around thinking, "I'm a genius, I'm a genius!" You will need ongoing encouragement and support for your unique genius abilities to manifest in a bigger way. This is the fundamental purpose of genius community.

Once you've assessed and identified your natural genius, you've only just begun. Don't be tempted back into your old insular universe. Introversion is one of the greatest threats to the ongoing expansion of your innate abilities. Just because you've beaten the demons of rejection once doesn't mean you're immune in the future.

None of us is such a superman or superwoman that we can stand on our own against the criticism and resistance of small-minded people. If you try to withstand this alone, you risk encapsulating yourself away from the world as a whole. You might think you're holding your ground, but by shutting down even the smallest amount, you are already in retreat. Because people cannot relate to you, you stop relating to people. You need the stimulation of the world to keep growing.

When you receive criticism and have no one to support your vision, you might think you're okay, but protection is the automatic response. You withdraw back into yourself. You think you can live your genius in the dark, but this is really not possible. You need the full light of day. Otherwise, your natural genius can turn dark itself and work against you. Create people around you that allow and encourage you to flourish out in the open. It takes genius to build and sustain natural genius. To continue developing yourself, you need to surround yourself with like-minded individuals and professionals.

Acceptance Without Conformity

The genius community is a community of peers. We do not mean any age group, tax bracket or profession; we mean fellow geniuses. You're not seeking superficial sameness. if you discriminate by race, age, religion, sexual preference, or any other social dividers, you might miss a natural genius. If you miss genius in others, you miss it in yourself.

When you can see innate genius abilities in other people, you become more in touch with your own organic excellence. This mirroring effect helps further clarify who you are inside and why you feel the passion that you feel. When you acknowledge someone else's genius, your own innate abilities are strengthened and nurtured.

The urge to copy someone else, or the urge to have yourself mimicked, is just another way to suppress genius, both your own and others' genius. A genius community invites the free expression of each individual for the evolution of their excellence. This is no small challenge. Acceptance without conformity rarely exists in our world, which helps account for the low manifestation of natural genius we currently experience.

To be perfectly clear, we are not talking about unconditional acceptance; that would be a disaster for a genius community. A genius community will only work if all members of the community share the vision to explore, unfold, apply and sharpen each person's innate abilities. If any members do not share this vision, no matter how intelligent or engaging they might be, they would only serve to distract the others.

A genius community needs people with a high level of personal integrity and common sense. These are people who've already begun to realize and apply their innate abilities in one form or another. Although everyone has genius written in their DNA, many of us are still disconnected from it. They are not yet ready to be part of the genius community, so you need to be selective without being exclusive.

Communication is the Key

The purpose of any solid genius community is to stimulate the continued growth and development of each member. So, there must be open lines of communication between everyone. If you can't be open, you cannot be a part of a genius community.

On the other hand, to maintain real openness between people, there must be a high level of mutual feeling and respect. Criticism will close people down, even if they don't want to do so. Shutting down is an automatic defense response.

A genius community develops a high level of communication, where people can be real without putting down one another. This requires seeing the genius in the other person at all times, no matter what they are going through.

Geniuses must be open to feedback that differs from what they expect. If we already knew everything about ourselves and the world, we wouldn't need anyone else. So make yourself available to hear unexpected input. Why settle for your own impression of what's happening when you can benefit from the 360-degree perspective of others?

As geniuses, we are highly passionate, and we love to think big. When channeled in the right direction, our amplified energy can create massive results. If we get going down the wrong course, however, we can really make a mess for ourselves. Everyone needs to be reeled in once in a while. We all, on occasion, need to be told that some fantastic impulse of ours isn't such a great idea, after all. Such feedback won't suppress your creativity. Instead, the input will only sharpen your genius by helping you remain on track with the core vision you've already shared with those around you.

In addition to helping you stay on course, other people can save you from repetition as well. If we find one thing that works well for us, we want to do it over and over again. That's not genius, and sometimes we need someone else to remind us of this.

Our brains tend to get stuck in ruts, as we learned about the inner terrorist. We may become comfortable with the way things are going and how we do things, but the world around us is constantly changing. A genius community can help identify when it's time to take on the challenge of meeting new needs for your genius, when it's time to recover our passion for new ideas.

Many extremely talented individuals don't lack the support from a genius community, but they aren't willing to receive it. They refuse to risk being vulnerable to the response of other people. The reality is that by operating only in the bubble of their own minds, they make themselves extremely vulnerable to all sorts of mistakes that could easily have been prevented if they had the right people around them.

You may be surprised by the amount and intensity of the praise you receive. For some people, this is harder to take than criticism. So, prepare to open up to encouragement by people who truly get who you are. Most of us have lived on crumbs of encouragement. Faced with a complete feast, we may feel like it's too much, but we need all the support we can get. We need fuel that feeds the engine of our excellence.

A genius community is not about determining right and wrong, so don't get sucked into debate and discussion. Go for personal expression about real experience. That is what moves us all to unfold our innate potential.

Make Your Life Easy: Anyone May Have the Next Big Idea

You are elite because you've chosen to explore and express your innate excellence. This commitment should be true of every person in the genius community, so it's a level playing field where everyone is royalty while no one is the king.

Geniuses often draw around them a court of admirers to whom they can play the role of king. The famed architect Frank Lloyd Wright serves as a good example of this. To his winter camp in Arizona, Taliesin West, he would draw apprentice architects, artists and musicians who collectively enriched the community. Wright was the undisputed king at Taliesin. Everything there occurred on his terms.

Wright surely was a genius, but his community was not. He attracted talented people, but they could only function under him. Taliesin West today is more of a memorial to Wright than a high-performing creative community. No matter how forward-looking the work, Wright's community wasn't looking ahead; it was looking at him.

In a true genius community, the next "big idea" could come from anyone. There is no need to conflict with leadership because no one is putting a lid on anyone else. This speeds up innovation in each individual and allows those pursuing very different professional activities to benefit from one another. You want fast paced and intense collaboration, not competition. Cooperation supports genius.

This understanding is critical because geniuses are intense people. When they fight, they can destroy as much or more than they've ever created. Some have mythologized this duality as essential to the creative process. Not so. Your innate abilities are yours and yours alone. It makes no sense whatsoever to pit your own excellence against someone else's. Let them do things their way, and you do things your way.

The great debates of art are an excellent example of this waste of genius. Folk, realism, abstract impressionism, traditional fine art, and contemporary art all have a rightful place. Rather than fighting over which is the most authentic way to paint, let each artist access what they feel in their gut and support each other to get on with it.

During one of our local genius community meetings, Laura shared an important insight. “I am excited to be connected with so many people who walk their talk,” she said. “I was tired of informal socializing and opinionated discussion in other circles. I am so glad I found this group with a receptive attitude, deep listening, and thoughtful speaking to nurture each others’ natural genius. I like especially how each person’s experience and inner thoughts help the group grow and expand. Thank you for leveraging all of the many talents inherent inside of the group.”

AFTERWORD

We hope you've enjoyed reading this book. More importantly, we hope you use these insights and principles to enhance your life dramatically. You need to step back from your current life and look at it through your new genius eyes.

Evaluate your life not just with your brain but also with your gut. Decide what your life will look like when it's finally the way you want it. Recognize the gap between where you are now and where you need to be – where your dream becomes a reality.

That gap tells you exactly what needs to be done to create the life of your dreams. If you look through your genius eyes, you will discover that the gap is always created by the absence of you living your genius 100 percent.

First and foremost, find out exactly what is your natural genius. You need total clarity about your unique combination of genius abilities before you take any further action. To end any confusion around your personal genius is truly priceless.

Over the past five years, Otto and I have developed a proven *Genius Mastery Process*. You receive your personal genius profile and strategies to translate it into day-to-day life. Holding your hand, we will walk you through the transition that might be the most scary and yet the most important shift you've made in your life.

For many years we've assisted individuals worldwide to discover their brilliance and enrich their life by living it. We'd love to do the same for you. You begin by accepting our invitation to take part in our Genius Mastery experience. You will learn how to cross the bridge from where you are to where you want to be. The Genius Mastery experience will take you to a place you have never been before, and it will feel like home.

To take your first step, simply complete the form at the back of this book and follow the instructions provided.

And remember...

You can talk about it,
or you can think about it,
but when you do something about it,
you will change your life!

Let's get started! Here are four easy ways to contact us:

1. Photocopy the last page of the book and fax your key frustrations to us at this number: 623-266-4079
2. Visit our website at: http://geniuscoaching.net
3. Email us to geniusbook@geniuscoaching.net
4. Call us directly at this number: 623-266-3923

We look forward to serving you.

Susanna Lange & Otto Siegel
Phoenix, Arizona
July, 2007

SUGGESTED READING

Chapter 1

Michael Gelb, *How to Think Like Leonardo da Vinci: Seven Steps to Genius Every Day* (New York: Random House, 1998)

Michael Gelb, *Discover Your Genius: How to Think Like History's Ten Most Revolutionary Minds* (New York: Quill, 2003)

Andrej Aleinikov, PhD, *Mega Creativity: Five Steps to Thinking Like a Genius* (Cincinnati, OH: F&W Publications, 2002)

Rosamunde Stone Zander, Benjamin Zander, *The Art of Possibility* (New York: Penguin, 2000)

Dick Richards, *Is Your Genius At Work?* (Mountain View, CA: Davies-Black , 2005)

Michael Michalko, *Cracking Creativity: The Secrets of Creative Genius* (Berkeley, CA: Ten Speed Press, 2001)

Chapter 2

Ernie J. Zelinski, *The Joy of Thinking Big: Becoming a Genius in No Time Flat* (Berkeley, CA: Ten Speed Press, 1998)

Malcolm Gladwell, *Blink: The Power of Thinking Without Thinking* (New York: Time Warner Book Group, 2005)

Malcolm Gladwell, *The Tipping Point: How Little Things Can Make a Big Difference* (New York: Bay Back Books, 2002)

Neil Fiore, *The Now Habit* (New York: Penguin Putnam Inc. 1988)

Chapter 3

Michael Gershon, *The Second Brain: Your Gut has a Mind of its Own* (New York: Harper Collins Publishers, 1998)

Angela Martin, *Practical Intuition: Practical Tools for Harnessing the Power of Your Instinct* (New York: Barnes & Noble, 2002)
Carla Hannaford, PhD, *Smart Moves: Why Learning is Not All in Your Head* (Marshall, NC: Great Ocean Publishers, 1995)
Gordon Wainwright, *Body Language* (Blacklick, OH: McGraw Hill, 2003)

Chapter 4

De Becker, *The Gift of Fear* (New York: Dell Publishing Group, 1998)
James O. Prochaska, *Changing for Good: A Revolutionary Six-Stage Program for Over-coming Bad Habits* (New York: Harper Collins, 2002)

Chapter 5

Samuel Deep, Lyle Sussman, *Yes You Can* (Jackson, TN: Perseus Books Group 1996)
Jan and Bob Davidson, *Genius Denied: How to Stop Wasting Young Minds* (New York: Simon and Schuster, 2004)
Barbara Sher, *I Could Do Anything - If I Only Knew What It Was* (New York: Dell, 1995)
Lynn Grabhorn, *Excuse Me, Your Life Is Waiting* (Charlottesville, VA: Hampton Roads, 2003)
Ronald D. Davis, *The Gift of Dyslexia* (New York: Berkeley Publishing, 1994)
Edward Hallowell, MD, John Ratey, MD, *Delivered from Distraction: Getting the Most out of Life with Attention Deficit Disorder* (New York: Random House, 2005)
Dr. Paul E. Dennison, *Switching On: The Whole Brain: Answer to Dyslexia* (Ventura, CA: Edu-Kinesthetics Inc., 1981)
Kate Kelly, *You Mean I Am Not Lazy, Stupid or Crazy* (New York: Simon & Schuster, 1996)
Harriet Lerner, *The Dance of Fear* (New York: Harper Paperbacks, 2005)
Tony Buzan, *Use Both Sides of Your Brain* (New York: Penguin Group, 1989)
Joyce Wycoff, *Mindmapping* (New York: The Berkeley Publishing Group, 1991)

Chapter 6

Bobby DePorter, *Quantum Success* (Oceanside, CA: Learning Forum, 2006)
Dr. Wayne W. Dyer, *The Power of Intention* (Carlsbad, CA: Hay House, 2002)
Jack Canfield, *The Success Principles* (New York: HarperCollins, 2005)

Chapter 7

Markus Buckingham, Donald Clifton, *Now, Discover Your Strengths* (New York: The Free Press, 2001)

Tom Rath, *StrengthsFinder 2.0* (New York: Gallup Press, 2007

Dan Baker, *What Happy People Know* (Emmaus, PA: Rodale Press, 2003)

Chapter 8

Ben Stein, *How To Ruin Your Life* (Carlsbad, CA: Hay House, Inc, 2002)

Carlene DeRoo, *What's Right With Me* (Oakland, CA: New Harbinger, 2006)

Kathryn D. Cramer, *Change the Way You See Everything* (New York: Penguin, 2006)

Bill L. Little, *Self Destruction Made Easy* (Gretna, LA: Pelican Publishing Company 2006)

Steve Chandler, *The Story of You* (New Jersey: Career Press, 2006)

Chapter 9

Seth Godin, *Stop Trying to Be Perfect and Start Being Remarkable* (New York: Penguin, 2006)

Adrian Slywotzky, *The Art of Profitability* (New York: Warner Books Inc., 2002)

Seth Godin, *Purple Cow: Transform Your Business by Being Remarkable* (New York: Penguin, 2002)

T. Harv Eker, *Secrets of the Millionaire Mind: Mastering the Inner Game of Wealth* (New York: Harper Collins, 2005)

Chapter 10

Stephen R. Covey, *The 7 Habits of Highly effective People* (New York: Free Press, 1990)

Stephen R. Covey, *The 8th Habit: From Effectiveness to Greatness* (New York: Free Press, 2004)

Stephen M.R. Covey, *The Speed of Trust: The One Thing That Changes Everything* (New York: Free Press, Simon & Schuster, 2006)

Jim Collins, *Good to Great: Why Some Companies Make the Leap and Others Don't* (New York: Harper Collins Publishers, 2001)

Kevin Freiberg, Jackie Freiberg, *Nuts! Southwest Airlines' Crazy Recipe for Business and Personal Success* (Austin, TX: Bard Press Inc., 1996)

Herb Baum, *The Transparent Leader: How to Build a Great Company Through Straight Talk, Openness, and Accountability* (New York: Harper Collins, 2004)

Michael J. Jones, Steve Sanghi, *Driving Excellence: How the Aggregate System Turned Microchip Technology from a Failing Company to a Market Leader* (Hoboken, NJ: John Wiley & Sons, Inc., 2006)

Daniel H. Pink, *A Whole New Mind: Moving From the Information Age to the Conceptual Age* (New York: Riverhead Books, 2005)

Chapter 11

Daniel Goleman, *Social Intelligence: the New Science of Human Relationship* (New York: Bantam Dell, 2006)

Warren Bennis, Patricia Ward Biedermann, *Organizing Genius* (Reading, MA: Perseus Books, 1997)

Bob Prosen, *Kiss Theory Good Bye* (Carrollton, TX: Gold Pen Publishing, 2006)

Jonathan Tisch, *The Power of We: Succeeding Through Partnerships* (Hoboken, NJ: John Wiley and Sons, 2004)

Julie Jansen, *You Want Me to Work With Who?* (Knowxville, TN: Penguin Non-Classics, Penguin Group, 2006)

German Books

Gaby Miketta, *Netzwerk Mensch: Einführung in die Psychoneuroimmunologie* (Hamburg: Rowolt Taschenbuch Verlag, 1994)

Sammy Molcho, *Körpersprache* (München: Mosaik Verlag, 1983)

Sammy Molcho, *Körpersprache im Beruf* (München: Goldmann Verlag, 2001)

Konrad Kunsch und Steffen Kunsch, *Der Mensch in Zahlen: Eine Datensammlung in Tabellen mit über 20,000 Einzelwerten* (Heidelberg: Spectrum Verlag, 2000)

Walter Russell, *Das Genie Steckt in Jedem* (Oberstaufen: Genius Verlag, 1998)

Yes, I want to take the first step into owning my genius!

Please have a genius coach contact me by telephone. I'd like to know more about how the Genius Mastery Program can help me implement the ideas in *Yes, You Are a Genius.*

My Key Frustrations:

- ☐ I don't know my genius.
- ☐ I have many ideas but don't know what to do first.
- ☐ I don't make enough money.
- ☐ I don't like what I now do.
- ☐ I could do much more, but I don't know what and how.
- ☐ I don't have the money to transition into a business that is based on my genius.
- ☐ I can live only a small percentage of my genius where I am at right now.
- ☐ My family doesn't support my genius.
- ☐ I see other people's talents but I am blind to my own.
- ☐ I feel burned out.
- ☐ I am always behind.
- ☐ I don't find many people who can keep up with me.
- ☐ I am frequently bored with myself or others.
- ☐ I can't sell myself.
- ☐ I have a hard time finding friends I feel close with.
- ☐ I never get what I really want.
- ☐ I am too much for most people.
- ☐ I don't have enough time.
- ☐ I am not recognized for who I really am.
- ☐ Other____________________

____
____
____
____
____

My Information:

Name ______________________________ Company Name ______________________________
Address ____
City ______________________________ State _____ Zip Code ______________
Email Address ____
Daytime Phone Number ____
Describe Your Current Profession ____
____ Years in Profession______

Three Easy Ways to Contact Us:

- Visit our website at http://geniuscoaching.net
- Photocopy and Fax this completed form to 623-266-4079
- Call Genius Coaching at 623-266-3923

Share the Gift of Genius

Order *Yes, You Are a Genius* for your family and friends!

(Hardback – ISBN-13: 978-0-9791102-0-7)

___# of Copies at $24.95 each for $_________ Total Due (Arizona residents add 8.1% tax)

Payment Method: ___Credit Card ___Debit Card ___Check ___Money Order

Card Authorization Information:

Card Type: ___MasterCard ___Visa ___American Express

Name on Card: ______________________________

Card Billing Address: ______________________________

City: ______________ State: __________ Zip: ______________

Card Number: ______________________________

Expiration Date: ________(mm/yy) Authorized Amount $_________ (e.g., $24.95)

Authorizing Signature: ______________________________

Shipping Information:

___Same as information above, or:

Name: ______________________________

Address: ______________________________

City: ______________ State: __________ Zip: ______________

Daytime Telephone Number: ______________________________

Four Easy Ways to Order *Yes, You Are a Genius*:

- Photocopy and Fax this completed form to 623-266-4079
- Order by phone (9-5 Pacific Time, M-F) at 623-266-3923
- Order online at http://geniuscoaching.net
- Mail to Genius Press, 3120 West Carefree Highway, Suite 1-413, Phoenix, AZ 85086.

GENIUS PRESS